BIRGER GERHARDSSON

The Gospel Tradition

CWK GLEERUP
1986

Published with grants from the Swedish Council for Research in the Humanities and Social Sciences.

CWK Gleerup is the imprint for the scientific and scholarly publications of Liber Förlag, Malmö, Sweden.

Abstract

Gerhardsson, B. 1986. The Gospel Tradition. Coniectanea Biblica. New Testament Series 15. 57 pp. Monograph. ISBN 91-40-05157-9.

The author presents herein a model for the investigation of tradition, addressing the issue in a more explicated manner than in his earlier writings. A basic distinction is made between "inner" and "outer" tradition, addressing four aspects of the latter: verbal, behavioural, institutional and material tradition. The model is first presented in phenomenological terms and then applied to Early Christianity's Jewish mother-tradition and to Early Christianity itself. The majority of the book is devoted to a discussion of the verbal tradition in Early Christianity, especially the gospel tradition. Attention is paid to such topics as text creation, oral and written transmission and the process of synthetization and writing down, among others. Issues deemed in need of additional research are delineated.

Key words: Tradition. Orality. Oral tradition. Gospel tradition. The synoptic question.

Printed by Wallin & Dalholm, Lund   ISBN 91-40-05157-9

Preface

April 7—23 1984 a symposium was held in Jerusalem: *Symposium de inter-relatione evangeliorum.* Penetrating discussions were devoted to the complicated question of the genetic relationships between the first three Gospels. The meeting had been well prepared in advance. Papers had been written by three research teams — each representing an important approach to the synoptic question (the two document hypothesis, the two Gospel hypothesis and the multiple stage hypothesis) — and by individual scholars who elucidated specific aspects of the overall problem. No limit was set for the length of the papers. They were distributed and read in advance, while at the symposium the discussions began immediately, following brief introductions. An important task for the meeting was to delineate areas for additional research.

The following presentation consists of my contribution to the symposium, somewhat improved. Its character is determined by the fact that it was written for this context. I thank the participants of the meeting for the rewarding discussions. Furthermore, I would like to express my gratitude to Professors Ben F. Meyer and Robert A. Guelich who made valuable suggestions for the amelioration of my manuscript, and to Professor Donald A. Hagner who polished my English.

Lund in April 1986

Birger Gerhardsson

Content

Introduction   9
1.   *A model of investigation*   11
1.1.   Survey   12
1.2.   Commentary   14
1.3.   Programmatic tradition and *de facto* tradition   15
2.   *Christianity's Jewish mother-tradition*   17
3.   *The Early Christian tradition*   20
3.1.   Survey   20
3.2.   Inner tradition   21
3.3.   Outer tradition   22
3.3.1.   Material tradition   22
3.3.2.   Institutional tradition   23
3.3.3.   Behavioural tradition   25
3.3.4.   Verbal tradition   28
3.3.4.1.   The information in the Lukan prologue   28
3.3.4.2.   Oral and written transmission   30
3.3.4.3.   The interaction between written and oral tradition   33
3.3.4.4.   Firm and flexible elements   34
3.3.4.5.   The origin and character of the gospel tradition   39
3.3.4.6.   The production of texts: creation, reshaping, compilation   42
3.3.4.7.   The synthetization of the text material   46
3.3.4.8.   The process of writing down   49
3.3.4.9.   The polyphonic character of the written gospel   53
3.3.4.10.   Holy writ and viva vox   56

Introduction

Our inclusive word "tradition" covers a complicated reality, a phenomenon so basic and omnipresent in human existence that a rational flouroscopy is difficult to make. The complex and partly elusive phenomenon of tradition is studied in many disciplines. Yet, it seems to be a fact that we still look in vain for works which collect and combine insights from all the different disciplines and try to make an all-comprehensive and synthetic description of the phenomenology of tradition: what tradition is and how it functions as an integrated totality and in all its aspects.[1]

Historically, Christianity may be characterized as a new tradition which originates within a well developed mother-tradition and gradually liberates itself from this; at the same time it also receives influences from other traditions in the milieu. This paper will deal with the gospel tradition, seen as part of the Early Christian tradition. Let me indicate the way I delimit my subject. Certainly I am going to mobilize insights from many areas and many disciplines but the historical sphere we shall directly deal with in this paper is Early Christianity in the New Testament period against its background in the Judaism of the centuries around the beginning of our time-reckoning and in its so-called "Hellenistic" surroundings. Within this area we shall study tradition in its most important aspects, especially "the gospel tradition". With the last designation — as well as with the name "the concrete Jesus-tradition" — I mean the tradition about the teaching, works and fate of Jesus during his life on earth (including the signs of his resurrection), *in concreto*, mainly tradition of the sort which has been compiled in the synoptic Gospels (and in a more decked-out form in the Gospel of John).

It seems to be possible to analyse and discuss the Early Christian (and the Jewish) tradition with the aid of a rather simple model of investigation which I will soon present. But let me first say that I am aware of the fact that further distinctions and classifications are possible and

---

[1] Cf., however, P.-G. Müller, *Der Traditionsprozess im Neuen Testament. Kommunikations-analytische Studien zur Versprachlichung des Jesusphänomens* (Freiburg, Basel, Wien: Herder, 1982) 11—111, and E. Shils, *Tradition* (London: Faber & Faber, 1981). — For literature on the gospel tradition, see R. Riesner, *Jesus als Lehrer. Eine Untersuchung zum Ursprung der Evangelien-Überlieferung* (WUNT 2.R., 7; 2nd ed.; Tübingen: Mohr, 1984) 503—68, 615.

desirable; however, such specifications belong to more penetrating analysis and specialized debate. I am also aware of the fact that my terminology is somewhat rough. It is, however, handy, and that is important even in scholarly discussions. Finally, I also know that my distinctions sometimes appear artificial, since tradition in its best stages is a rather well integrated, organically coherent entity. Yet, I intend my distinctions to be realistic: very commonly the different aspects of tradition are disjoined and the different elements exist separately. We do need a convenient term for each one of them.

One of my purposes is to emphasize *questions* where further research and discussion are desirable. I shall mention here a very great number of such questions, old and new, and put a special stress on some of them. The "answers" I sketch very briefly are primarily meant as illustrations of the model of investigation and of the problems; as solutions of complicated problems they are rather approximate and preliminary.

I am a Christian, brought up in the Lutheran tradition. Certain proclivities and accents will presumably reveal that. And in no way do I reject different attempts to clarify the Early Christian tradition from confessional points of departure. In his book *Der Traditionsprozess im Neuen Testament* (1981), Paul-Gerhard Müller has made an insightful and many-sided analysis of the (verbal) New Testament tradition from a Catholic standpoint. Similar works ought to be done from non-Catholic positions as well. However, the approach I present here is not founded on any specific theological basis. Apart from certain outlooks and by-the-way comments, I here tackle the problem of tradition by means of secular scholarship. While this facilitates discussion with non-theological disciplines, I want to point out, on the other hand, that my approach leads to bad theology if naïvely developed into a New Testament theology. In an *historical* study of the origin and first development of Christianity one must consider the earth-bound human reality with its whole mixture of conflicting elements, shortcomings, compromises and the like. If, on the other hand, a *New Testament theology* shall be able to give a fresh picture of Early Christianity's message and content of faith, it cannot begin in the outer, earthly dimensions but must take the eruptive center of the message itself, as its starting point, i.e. those views and perspectives that filled Jesus and his followers and created Early Christianity: "The Reign of Heaven", Christ, the gospel — as preached and believed.

1. A model of investigation

It is my conviction that historical research must try to make very *concrete* reconstructions of the past, preferably in the form of vivid, visual pictures of the complex realities. The sources do not always allow that. But we can often advance rather far in the right direction if we apply, on the one hand, general ("phenomenological") insights about the way in which human beings function both individually and communally, and, on the other hand, special insights from that historical sphere in which the object of research is situated and from the analogies closest to it.

For the study of the Early Christian tradition we need a model of investigation. I have used one such model (with increasing clearness) in my works on the problem of tradition.[2] This model makes it possible to dissect the complicated phenomenon of Early Christian tradition, to elucidate its different aspects in congruent ways, to keep in mind the most important of them in the analyses of the texts, and to discuss the problems involved in a handy language.

The model is based on general "phenomenological" insights gained in many areas, times and disciplines, but it is specifically constructed for a study of the *Early Christian tradition* connected with its historical milieus, especially its *Jewish mother-tradition*. I shall here present it briefly but yet in a more developed and explicated way than I have done before.[3] The model is simple: a basic distinction is made between "inner" and "outer" tradition, and, within the outer tradition four separate aspects are to be noted: verbal, behavioural, institutional and material tradition.

In the following I shall first present the model of investigation in general, phenomenological terms and then more concretely show what it means when applied to the mother-tradition of Christianity and to

---

[2] *Memory and Manuscript. Oral Tradition and Written Transmission in Rabbinic Judaism and Early Christianity* (ASNU 22; Lund: Gleerup, Copenhagen: Munksgaard, 1961; 2nd ed. 1964), *Tradition and Transmission in Early Christianity* (ConNT 20; Lund: Gleerup, Copenhagen: Munksgaard, 1964), *The Origins of the Gospel Traditions* (Philadelphia: Fortress, London: SCM, 1979), Der Weg der Evangelientradition, *Das Evangelium und die Evangelien. Vorträge vom Tübinger Symposium 1982* (WUNT 28; ed. P. Stuhlmacher; Tübingen: Mohr, 1983) 79—102. In the following I will make frequent reference to these writings in order to indicate the continuity and development of my work on the problem of tradition, in the hopes of eliminating any existing misunderstandings of my position.
[3] See *Memory* 71—78, 290—94, *Tradition* 7, *Origins* 11—14, 31—32.

Early Christianity itself. Then I shall discuss the different aspects in somewhat more detail in relation to Early Christianity. The main stress will be laid upon the gospel tradition.

1.1. Survey

A. *Inner tradition.* When tradition functions ideally, it is animated, it "lives". It is carried and kept together by an inner engagement, by belief, convictions, values, views. An ideal traditionist is like a torch that lights other torches, some rabbis used to say.

A vital content of mind cannot remain locked up in the individual. It expresses itself in the fellowship, it becomes a "message" which is communicated to other people, it spreads to the environment and to next generation, if it is strong. It generates tradition. The decisive, "living" part of this, however, is difficult to analyse and describe. The words we use to indicate that one human being influences others are rather vague. We say that he "inspires" others, "convinces" others, "dominates" others, is "contagious" and so on. This is a kind of communication — a handing over and a receiving; therefore the word tradition is appropriate: "inner tradition". It is of course necessary to study the inner tradition but it is not easy. As an object of research it is elusive and difficult to grasp as is "life" itself: it is mobile, includes changes and variations, some parts grow, other parts decline, renewal occurs and "death". An analysis — which I am not going to do here — must include many aspects: cognitive, emotive, and volitional aspects, maybe more.

What is easier to come to grips with is the outward forms the inner tradition assumes. It not only expresses itself in a mental way, it also *externalizes* itself in visible and audible outward forms. These I call "outer tradition".

B. *Outer tradition.* The outward forms of a tradition can be of many kinds. For our purpose it seems to be enough that we specify four such forms or "dimensions":

(1) *Verbal tradition* (word-tradition). Non-verbally inner tradition finds expression in inarticulate sounds, glances, mimicry, movements of head, gestures with the hands, pointing and signing with the fingers and other forms of "body-language". But the communication acquires quite another precision when language is used, when verbal communication and verbal transmission occurs. By verbal tradition I mean words, utterances, texts, writings etc., which articulate the content of the inner tradition (both its old and its new elements). I do not only mean firm formulas and texts but also the free, flexible elements that are used in order

to express the content of tradition. Basically the verbal tradition is oral. In cultures where writing has had an influencial position, for a long time, the oral language is, however, often more or less clearly structured according to patterns of the written language; here the interaction between the written and the spoken word is a very interesting problem.

Language plays an immensely vital role for almost all efficient transmission of tradition.[4] Certainly human beings can hand over much to each other and to future generations without words, but normally language plays a key role in most kinds of transmission of tradition. With language we can fix a content of mind, take care of it in an effective way and spread it through a communication which is more distinct and explicit than other forms of outer tradition. As a rule the different forms of outer tradition interplay but the verbal tradition is without doubt the most influential of them all. With the aid of language we can steer the course of tradition, indicate the programmatic center of it, make distinctions and specifications, revise or alter it, and so on.

(2) *Behavioural tradition* (practical tradition). The inner life of humans expresses itself in different behaviours as well. A prominent, influential human being transmits consciously and unconsciously his way of appearing and acting to others. A basic mechanism is the fact that spontaneously we imitate those humans we look up to, venerate, admire and love. The authoritative, admired human being is a "message" *per se*. Parents, teachers, masters and other "impressive" men or women become pattern-forming. We speak of "the force of the example" and, with the awareness thereof, demand that persons in official position be irreproachable and "set good examples". Presumably this mechanism of imitation often corresponds to the proclivity of the influential individual to externalize himself forcefully in the fellowship, come forward from obscurity and silence, assert his influence, get his own way, "set the tone" or whatever we may call it. In this way the programmatic part of the behavioural tradition tends to concentrate on that which the influential individuals want to pass on.

(3) *Institutional tradition*. Vital inner tradition creates — in any case if it is of a religious nature — engagement and fellowship. And every human community organizes itself and institutionalizes itself. The process starts immediately. A fellowship is formed and a gulf begins growing between insiders and outsiders; and furthermore, within the former role-division, hierarchy and organization develop. If this did not happen, the members would be nothing but isolated individuals, only loose-

---

[4] Müller writes: "Keine Tradition funktioniert nämlich ohne Sprache"; *Traditionsprozess* 15. For my part I would not go that far.

13

ly connected to each other, and the group would soon be dissolved. To create coherent community these mechanisms are necessary: social fellowship, order, organization, structures, establishments.[5] A long experience tells us also that such phenomena are hard to destroy once they have developed, and difficult to change or abolish. — This I call "institutional tradition".

(4) *Material tradition* ("thing"-tradition). It is reasonable that we also discern a fourth form of outer tradition. The inner tradition often needs to use inanimate objects as means: specific localities, special clothes, tools or other outward equipment, vital for the efficient function of tradition. This we may designate as "material tradition".[6]

1.2. Commentary

In the ideal case these different aspects function in interaction. The carriers, filled by the inner tradition, effectively make use of the different parts of the outer tradition. New members are won and socialized into this multi-dimensional tradition. When this process is successful, the new tradition is *internalized* in the new member so that he becomes a genuine and "living" traditionist himself. In such cases the differentiation of aspects may appear somewhat artificial.

But the situation is not often an ideal one. The different aspects of a rich tradition do not belong together *by necessity:* they must *be kept* together by an inner engagement. And they are different even in regard to mobility and flexibility. The inner tradition may be very mobile — develop, change, be renewed — without the outward forms being able to keep pace with it. The outer forms have a stiffness and firmness, which the inner tradition does not have. *Intra muros* some people may accept parts of the outer tradition but not all of it, and they may even adopt most of the outer tradition without acquiring the living inner engagement. *Extra muros* an outsider can come across single, isolated elements from this tradition: get an inanimate object in his hand without knowing how to use it, meet forms of organization that he can do nothing but wonder about, see behaviour that appears meaningless to him, hear words that he cannot understand. This shows that it is meaningful in an investigation to separate the different aspects so that we can speak about them one by one when necessary (often it is not at all necessary).

[5] See B. Holmberg, *Paul and Power. The Structure of Authority in the Primitive Church as Reflected in the Pauline Epistles* (ConBNT 11; Lund: Gleerup, 1979), (Philadelphia: Fortress, 1980).
[6] In my earlier writings (cf. n. 3 above) I have not isolated "material tradition" as a specific aspect but included it in the "institutional tradition".

I should perhaps mention two more observations of a general kind. The outward forms of tradition are — when they emerge — motivated and more or less *necessary*. Otherwise they would not arise so regularly. But they are also *problematic*. First, they are as a rule conventionalizing elements as such. Few people can verbalize their inward experiences in totally adequate words, least of all their deepest and most overwhelming experiences. Few people can create new words, expressions, texts. We must more or less all make use of linguistic means which already exist, when we shall verbalize our experiences and communicate them to others. Already at the first verbalization the original content of mind becomes domesticated and conventionalized to some extent.

The same applies to our behaviour. Few people are radically creative in their behaviour and actions. Already existing patterns are taken into use as models, with minor or major alterations. Even as to organization and institutional forms human imagination is limited; in addition we are dominated by certain general mechanisms of a socio-psyhological character. Social organization and institutionalized forms are seldom radically new. A new movement must as a rule content itself with existing forms in its first phase. This fact reduces its possibility of being original. In all dimensions we see that the outer forms of tradition are intrinsically more or less domesticating and conventionalizing factors.

Second, outer tradition has a general tendency to exist on its own and run idly. These firm forms can be in use even when there is no inward engagement behind them. And once they are well established they generally are very difficult to reform or exchange. Therefore, they usually keep their form a long time even when the inner tradition has developed and changed so as to require altered or new outward forms. The history of religion is full of pious words and texts, which many people take to their lips but only few follow in life and action; rites, habits and customs which long ago lost their original rationale but are still practiced; institutional forms which go on in their beaten tracks in spite of the fact that they hinder rather than serve their original aims; things outdated and unfit which should have been discarded centuries ago but are still in use. Summa: inner tradition needs outer tradition but the later is always problematic; it must be under permanent supervision if it shall continue to be an adequate tool for the inner tradition.

1.3. Programmatic tradition and de facto tradition
No new tradition makes all things new. Emotionally it can be felt so, the mottos can run so, but in real life a new tradition initially changes

nothing but a small, illuminated circle within the existing realities.[7] If, however, the new tradition is strong and vital, it widens its area successively: ever more of the inherited realities are taken up in the light of new awareness and made the object of consideration and decision, with or without alterations.

In order to keep this in mind one must, I think, make a distinction between programmatic tradition and *the facto* tradition. The former designation stands for that which is new or penetrated by the new tradition, the latter for the immense older tradition which is still there without having been consciously accepted or consciously rejected.

The *de facto* tradition is of interest from many angles, not only as the mother-womb which has given birth to the new tradition and as the mother-breast on which it can live for a long time. An important problem is the fact that even leading representatives of the new tradition may spread much older, uncontrolled *de facto* tradition: they practice old values and behaviour which they have not contemplated and spread them without being aware of it.

In the sources, *de facto* tradition is difficult to come to grips with. That which is common and self-evident is only mentioned by accident in the sources. In contrast the sources provide an effective witness about the programmatic tradition: one is occupied with this, one speaks about this. This fact is especially evident when the traditionists expressly indicate that this shall be observed and maintained as tradition: $\varphi\upsilon\lambda\acute{\alpha}\sigma\sigma\epsilon\iota\nu$, $\tau\eta\varrho\epsilon\tilde{\iota}\nu$, $\iota\sigma\tau\acute{\alpha}\nu\alpha\iota$, $\kappa\alpha\tau\acute{\epsilon}\chi\epsilon\iota\nu$, $\kappa\varrho\alpha\tau\epsilon\tilde{\iota}\nu$, etc.[8] Even summons to take heed, listen, "see and hear", and the like, are telling, as are exhortations to receive and accept.

---

[7] Cf. *Tradition* 22—23.
[8] Cf. O. Cullmann, *Die Tradition als exegetisches, historisches und theologisches Problem* (Zürich: Zwingli, 1954) 12—16, *Memory* 288—91, and *Origins* 25—28.

2. Christianity's Jewish mother-tradition

In its first formative period, Early Christianity received influences from many corners. It would, however, be a serious historical mistake to put these influences on the same level. One of them must be placed in a class by itself and called the mother-tradition of Christianity. Jesus, the twelve and almost every man in a leading position in the first decades of Early Christianity were Jews by birth and upbringing, being socialized in the Jewish tradition. Jesus confined himself almost exclusively to the Jewish population of Palestine, and the Early Christian mission was primarily directed to Jews or proselytes — and other people who were already attracted by Judaism. Christianity was born within Judaism. Neither Jesus nor the Church in its first decades ever wanted to be anything else than Israel: they looked upon themselves as the *true* Israel. Their message presented news from Israel's God: what he now wanted to do and what he now had to say to his people — in a new time. In one way we could say that the original Christian message can be regarded as a concentration and radicalization of the ancient belief within the covenant between Israel and its God.

Early Christianity initially felt at home in Judaism and from it inherited considerable inhibitions and reservations to other cults and everything which was connected with them: paganism, heathenism! Therefore we have all reason to call the Judaism of antiquity Early Christianity's "mother-tradition". This must not prevent a full consideration of the fact that the Jews were "Hellenized" to a considerable degree at this time, even the Jews in Palestine. Nor must it prevent us from seeing the influences from different "Hellenistic" traditions that had their impact upon Christian communities none the less during the decades — and centuries — which followed.

Let us now apply our model to ancient Judaism, let us say from 200 BC to AD 200.

A. *Inner tradition.* The Jews in Palestine at the beginning of our Christian era constituted a relatively pluralistic society. Yet, it does not seem farfetched to speak of "Judaism" at that time — they even had themselves the designation Ἰουδαϊσμός[9] — and to take the pious, religiously active

---

[9] E.g. 2 Mack 2:21, 8:1, 14:38. Cf. Gal 1:13, 14. Note that the term is used in the singular; "Judaisms" is a modern manner of speaking.

Jews as the most representative Jews, in any case when we are looking for the mother-tradition of Christianity. To these Jews Jewish identity and inherited tradition in its totality was a programmatic concern, the Torah-tradition in all its aspects.

This Jewish tradition was immensely rich and multifarious. Yet, it had a vital inner life: the Torah-centric relation to "the only true God" with its different elements: faith, love, obedience, loyalty in emotions, thought, word, action towards God and a corresponding attitude to fellow human beings. To the pious representatives of the Torah-tradition this was a conscious program. They wanted to stand in covenant with God, and tradition showed what this covenant meant in its different aspects. As to Israel as a people, the Temple, the synagogues, the schools and other institutions were devoted to God and revealed his gifts and his demands.[10] As to the individual pious man, the centre of the covenant and the Torah-tradition is made clear to him, when twice a day he actualizes to himself the covenant by reading the Shema'. First he "takes the yoke of the Reign of Heaven" upon himself by affirming God's sovereign position as the only true God with the words: "The Lord our God, the Lord is one Lord". Then he takes upon himself "the yoke of the commandments", all of them in condensed form, by accepting the claim that he shall love the Lord his God with his whole heart, his whole soul and all his resources. Before Him who is One, God's people and every member of it shall be one. Here, as in many other ways, we see the program that everything shall be put under the grace and will of God and that the individual as well as the people shall accept all of it. Thus, a strong tendency toward unity is characteristic for the leading representatives of the Torah-tradition.[11]

Of course we must consider the *de facto* pluralism in Israel when trying to make a careful detailed description of the situation. How much of the rich heritage had at this time been consciously taken into the enlightened spot, invented and regulated? How many of the Jews did in fact accept this program whole-heartedly and in all its breadth? Where shall we put the tepid Jews? Uneducated Jews? People in isolated areas? And so forth. But these are common problems irrespective of what model we choose.

B. *Outer tradition.* (1) *Verbal tradition.* In the ancient Jewish tradition language plays an accentuated role; seeing and visions are not so much in the forefront as are words, speaking, and hearing. The Torah-tradition

---

[10] Cf. *Memory* 71—78. See also Riesner, *Jesus* 97—245.

[11] For literature on the role of the Shema' in early Judaism and early Christianity, see *Origins* 93—94.

was passed on with the aid of a rich treasure of authoritative terms, expressions, formulas, motifs, texts and writings, preserved in an oral and written tradition with both firm and flexible elements: Torah as words. (I do not take "Torah" in the narrow sense "law" but in its wider sense "teaching": all that which was classified as God's authoritative teaching to his people, directly or indirectly.[12] And I repeat once more that this word-tradition had a large *flexible* sector.[13])

(2) *Behavioural tradition.* "The life in the Torah" (ἡ ἔννομος βίωσις, Sir prol 14) was eminently an inherited, characteristic way of life, conscious patterns for the way in which the people and different groups and individuals should live: rites, customs, ethos, halacha. Here we meet Torah as practice.[14]

(3) *Institutional tradition.* The faithful Jews also maintained a rich inheritance of institutions and establishments, social structures, hierarchy, official divisions of role and more of the same. Even this was accepted as ordered by God; this was Torah as institution.

(4) *Material tradition.* The Torah-tradition finally included sacred localities, clothes, tools and other outward things: the Temple, the synagogues, scrolls, phylacteries, tassels on cloaks etc., things of importance for life in the Torah. If the expression can be allowed, I would like to call it "Torah as things".

---

[12] Even in *Memory* I did not take the word "Torah" in the narrow meaning "law", nor "oral Torah" in the narrow meaning "the halacha-rules". This seems to have escaped J. Neusner, in spite of the fact that it is stated and motivated rather clearly in the first chapter of *Memory*, 19—32; it is even printed in italics: "*In this investigation we shall use the term Torah, without qualification, as a collective designation for the Jew's sacred authoritative tradition (doctrine) in its entirety*"; 21. I also tried to clear away any misunderstanding about this in *Tradition* 7. Torah does not contain texts alone, nor are all texts legal rules. Again, my designation "verbal tradition" not only covers texts but all other authoritative teaching expressed in words as well, even flexible words; "verbal" means here "articulated" (see *Tradition* 7). In addition: When I say that the written Torah must always have had oral Torah at its side, I do not mean that Moses received the Rabbinic halacha-rules on Sinai but simply that no law-maker can express *everything* in his brief written rules. From the very beginning the text needs oral complements, exposition, and additional teaching. I regret that Neusner, who has clarified important aspects of the Rabbinic halacha-tradition so brilliantly (cf. below n. 70), has presented *my* position as if I was an old Jewish fundamentalist, believing that the halacha-rules of the tannaitic and amoraic Rabbis were received by Moses on Sinai in their present form; see e.g. Neusner, *The Rabbinic Traditions about the Pharisees before 70* (3 vols; Leiden: Brill, 1971) 3. 146—48, 163—77, and The Rabbinic Traditions about the Pharisees before 70 A.D.: The Problem of Oral Tradition, *Kairos* 14 (1972) 57—70.
[13] See above n. 12 and below nn. 44 and 57.
[14] For an illustration, see *Memory* 181—89.

3. The Early Christian tradition

We now will see in what way our model separates different aspects within the Early Christian tradition. Let me start with a brief survey.

3.1. Survey

A. *Inner tradition.* The heart of Early Christianity was a Jesus Christ-centered relation of God: faith, love, obedience, loyalty etc., and a corresponding attitude to fellow human beings.

B. *Outer tradition.* (1) *Verbal tradition.* The programmatic speaking of Early Christianity has a centre: Jesus Christ, interpreted as the decisive, final Saviour and Lord. One speaks about him, preaches about him, teaches about him, quotes sayings from him and tells narratives about him. Texts arise, some very firm, some more or less flexible. Gradually, smaller or larger written records are made, and letters are written about his mysteries. As time goes on more comprehensive writings are composed. In a living interaction we meet here firm and flexible elements with all kinds of intermediate forms: the Christ-tradition as words.

(2) *Behavioural tradition.* Linked up with inherited Jewish behavioural tradition and in its centre dominated by the practice and teaching of Jesus, Early Christianity develops a characteristic way of life. It is rich and variegated but it is very revealing that the program for the adherents of Jesus is called "the life in Christ", "following Jesus" or "imitation of Christ". Here we meet the Christ-tradition as practice.[15]

(3) *Institutional tradition.* Jesus attracts a central group of adherents, binds them to his person and becomes their exclusive leader and inspirer. A delimited group is formed around him and an elementary organization starts developing. After the departure of the exclusive master this group must be reconstructed and reorganized. This hastens the process of institutionalization; division of roles, hierarchy and organization develops. The Christ-tradition gets institutional forms.

---

[15] E. Larsson, *Christus als Vorbild. Eine Untersuchung zu den paulinischen Tauf- und Eikontexten* (ASNU 23; Lund: Gleerup, Copenhagen: Munksgaard, 1962), E. Cothenet, Imitation du Christ, *Dsp* fasc. 48—49 (1970) 1536—82.

(4) *Material tradition.* When it goes about outward things the Jesus-movement and the young Church do not need any specifically new things at the beginning. They take what they need from the mother-tradition. Not until later does the specifically Christian material tradition become interesting.

3.2. Inner tradition

Looking backward historically, we see that Jesus initiates a new tradition in the bosom of the Jewish mother-tradition. It is not difficult to understand that this historical volcanic eruption begins as an inner tradition; a strong conviction of faith and a firm consciousness of vocation makes Jesus turn to the community — "to appear publicly before Israel" — in order to influence his people with words and deeds. Within the mother-tradition — "the convenant" — he concentrates on the basic statements about God and his mighty deeds and proclaims to his people that God soon will take power in a new way. It will soon be seen what it means that God is God: the Lord is One and only One is the Lord. In this perspective he calls his people to repentance and inculcates the other side of the matter: God's people shall love God with their whole heart and their whole soul and all their resources.[16]

The demand that the community and the individual shall be "perfect" in their inner life (their "heart") and thus undivided, whole and without blemishes and defects before God was a basic ideal in the mother-tradition but Jesus accentuated it with a new radicalism. We then notice that the dominant men in the young Church share this engagement with its total demands. Certainly, Luke's notice in Acts 4:32 paints a very idealized picture of the Christian mother-community in Jerusalem, but the words are telling: "the whole company of those who believed were of one heart and one soul, and no one said that any of the things which he possessed was his own, but they had everything in common".[17] Many passages in the New Testament documents stress the demands for unity and consistency: one shall be a Christ-centred worshipper of God in everything. And the communities shall be united and unanimous in spite of a legitimate variety, inspired by one and the same Spirit, have one mind, "think the same" and so-forth.[18]

[16] For literature on these themes in the gospel tradition, see *Origins* 93—94.

[17] See my article Einige Bemerkúngen zu Apg 4,32, *ST* 24 (1970) 142—49.

[18] See e.g. Acts 2:44—47, 4:32, Rom 12:3—13, 15:5—6, 1 Cor 1:10—13, 12:4—31, Eph 4:1—16, Phil 1:27, 2:1—4, 3:15—16, Col 3:14—15 — not to speak of ethical texts like Matt 5:17—48. See further my book *The Ethos of the Bible* (Philadelphia: Fortress, 1981, London: Darton, Longman & Todd, 1982).

If one is aware of the complexity of the problems and the potential complications, it is thus possible to regard Early Christianity as a new tradition with an eruptive centre of inner tradition which expresses itself in words and behaviour, forms a new fellowship with an inceptive institution very early and which in the long run also has its consequences as to outward things.

Of course the most important question concerns the character and content of the inner tradition, but I cannot stop to discuss this matter now.[19]

3.3. Outer tradition

As we shall deal at length with "the gospel tradition" I shall comment on the verbal tradition last, despite the fact that in so doing the four aspects of outer tradition come in reverse order.

3.3.1. Material tradition

The theme "Early Christianity and material tradition" is a fascinating subject, still not very well clarified: what role did the Temple, the synagogues, Torah-scrolls, phylacteries and the like play for Jesus and Early Christianity; how did the development go, and how did Early Christianity's own material tradition evolve? We must of course consider the various components separately and also distinguish between different persons, groups, geographic areas and phases in the development of Early Christianity. The attitudes varied. Those who had pronouncedly spiritualized views and regarded Christianity as a "worship in spirit and truth" and those who remained faithful attenders at the Temple and synagogue with sustained respect for phylacteries etc., can not all be treated alike. Pauline and Johannine areas were not totally similar, nor do the oldest Pauline letters and the Pastoral letters reflect the same situation.

Telling is the strong difference between the Christians' attitude to the religious material tradition among the Jews and their attitude to things connected with pagan cults and pagan sacred practices.

In general I think we can say that the attitude to Jewish material tradition is a combination of familiarity, freedom and incipient liberation. The crux of the matter is the fact that the inner tradition generated great freedom towards all outward things, even the most religious ones. One

---

[19] I have tried to do so in other connections; see the literature mentioned in *Origins* 93—94.

·could do equally well with them or without them. Certainly the Christian Jews mourned when the Temple fell, but their own divine service was not interrupted. Certainly it was extremely distressing for them to leave the synagogue fellowship when this became necessary, but their own worship could continue just the same; the choice of some other room was no matter of principle. How the Christian Jews stopped using phylacteries, tassels and the like we do not even know. The development was obviously so undramatic that no source has noticed it.

Of course, a development in the direction towards a specifically Christian material tradition started quite early. Certain things gradually became sacred; localities with certain furnishings, clothes, eucharistic vessels etc. But we do not see much of this in the New Testament.

Of special interest is the question of the attitude to holy books, both as holy writ and as sacred things. Jesus and the leading men in Early Christianity probably ascribed to the opinion that the ancient holy scriptures should be treated with veneration, even as scrolls. Nothing indicates, however, that the writings and books produced by Early Christianity itself were immediately regarded as holy scriptures, even less as sacred things. Possibly the Book of Revelation is an exception (see 1:1—3, 22: 18—19). If notebooks were used, they were simply private means, not holy scriptures. They are not even mentioned in the New Testament. The books of which we catch a glimpse are the ancient holy scriptures. The written Gospels — presumably written in codex form — were not initially regarded as holy scriptures or sacred books. This did not come until later.

I shall not linger on this. However, I will stress once more that this aspect — material tradition — is also of importance for a realistic historical picture of the gospel tradition during the first century.

3.3.2. Institutional tradition

Jesus and Early Christianity lived in a world which was well institutionalized: politically, economically, socially, religiously: from the greatest structures of the Roman Empire down to the individual families, Jewish and non-Jewish alike. Jesus and the Christians were dependent upon this and accepted very much of it.[20] To the extent that

---

[20] From a theological point of view one thing is especially interesting in this connection: the fact that Jesus and his followers consciously refrained from making *political* responsibility their own specific cause. They presupposed that the different political rulers had a mission from God, which Jesus did not want to take from them: God's "secular realm" (Luther)!

these different institutions were of any importance to Early Christianity's programmatic tradition, we must take them into consideration. The attitudes to these different institutions, in principle and in practice, and the degree of radicalism and conservatism in relation to them need to be studied in order to gain an adequate picture of the Early Christian tradition.

More important for our investigation of the gospel tradition, however, is the process of institutionalization within Early Christianity itself. Two things are especially interesting:

(1) Jesus not only attracts throngs of people who listen to him accidentally or for some short period, and sympathizers at various places in Palestine. He gathers around himself a number of persons who become his "primary group": they "are with" him (εἶναι μετά), they "follow" him (ἀκολουθεῖν), they are his "disciples" (μαθηταί), they are his "brother and sister and mother".[21] This information in our sources is extremely important from a "phenomenological" point of view. We recognize the pattern: the strong and exclusive gathering around Jesus creates an incipient gulf between insiders and outsiders, a gulf which becomes even more pronounced when the Jesus-movement is reconstructed after Easter.

(2) Within this primary group emerges an embryonic organization: a certain ranking order becomes natural, a certain distribution of roles etc. Twelve disciples have a special position as a kind of symbolical collegium around the master; three of them constitute an inner circle and one of these is the primus. It seems to me very likely that Jesus himself took the initiative to organize in this elementary fashion his closest adherents. Even if he did not, it is easy to explain that this organization originated very soon in the most permanent fellowship around him; that is the way fellowship generally behaves!

If we consider this fact — institutional tradition in Early Christianity — we can be rather sure as to one thing. The followers of Jesus — before and after his departure — did not think that the truth about their master was to be found among the outsiders. Of course, rumours were spread about Jesus. Even if our sources did not say a word to that effect, we

---

[21] Examples: εἶναι μετά, Mark 3:14, 5:18, 14:67, Matt 26:69, 71, Luke 22:59; εἶναι σύν, Luke 8:38, 22:56; ἀκολουθεῖν, Mark 1:18, 2:14, 8:34, 10:21, 28, Matt 4:20, 22, 8:19, 22, 9:9, 10:38, 16:24, 19:21, 27, 28, Luke 5:11, 27, 28, 9:23, 57, 59, 61, 18:22, 28, John 1:43, 8:12, 12:26, 21:19, 22, ἔρχεσθαι ὀπίσω, Mark 8:34, Matt 10:38, 16:24, Luke 9:23, 14:27; cf. also δεῦτε ὀπίσω, Mark 1:17, Matt 4:19. "My brother, sister and mother", Mark 3:31—35, Matt 12:46—50, Luke 8:19—21. Note the expression ἔννομος Χριστοῦ in 1 Cor 9:21.

should be rather sure that rumours went out (διαφημίζειν) and that many people heard about the fame of Jesus (ἡ ἀκοὴ Ἰησοῦ).[22] But our knowledge about the way institutionalization functions teaches us that an engaged and structured religious community does not think much of outsider rumours and talk. What has authority is that which is cultivated *intra muros:* here the true insights are to be found. And here, inside the walls, all do not enjoy the same authority. Some have a reputation of being especially well informed, and a preference for "those in the know" is general in a fellowship.[23] Simple phenomenological insights tell us that those in the best position to spread recollections and traditions about Jesus within Early Christianity were those who had the reputation of being well informed, especially those who could say that they had seen with their own eyes and heard with their own ears. (A curious fact in contemporary New Testament scholarship is that the synoptic tradition cries out for actual originators but most leading scholars show very little proclivity for suspecting the twelve or other people with first-hand knowledge of Jesus.)[24]

3.3.3. Behavioural tradition

I am very much in doubt that any nation in the world can compete with the Jewish people in awareness and sophistication of their own way of life in every detail. The development in that direction had reached very far even in New Testament times. A strong political threat from different forces of occupation and a powerful spiritual and cultural threat from the flourishing Hellenistic culture had made the Jews observant and sensitive and evoked a remarkable zeal to defend Jewish identity and tradition — ὁ Ἰουδαισμός — in all its aspects, and not least the Jews' characteristic way of life with its many rules for religion and morality: rites, customs, ethos, halacha.

---

[22] Cf e.g. Mark 1:45, Matt 9:31; 28:15 (διαφημίζειν); Mark 1:28, Matt 4:24, 14:1 (ἀκοή).
[23] Some revealing New Testament texts: John 15:26—27, 19:35, 21:24, Luke 1:1—4, 24: 44:49, Acts 1:1—3, 8, 21—26, 2:32, 4:19—20, 5:15—16, 29—32, etc., 1 Cor 15:5—8, 11, 2 Cor 11:5, 12:11, Gal 1:18—20, 2:1—10 etc.
[24] In his article *Episkopē* and *episkopos:* the New Testament Evidence, *TS* 41 (1980) 322—38, R. Brown concludes concerning the twelve: "The image of them as carrying on missionary endeavors all over the world has no support in the NT or in other reliable historical sources. The archeological and later documentary evidence that Peter died at Rome is credible, but the rest of the Twelve could have died in Jerusalem so far as we have trustworthy information"; 325. — I think it is very proper indeed to ask the question: What did this highly reputed collegium actually *do* during its many years in Jerusalem?

Certainly the degree of awareness, enlightenment and actual observance shifted very much within pluralistic Judaism: from individual to individual, group to group, stratum to stratum, area to area. From this point of view the disciples of Jesus presumably had rather different backgrounds. The diversity was even greater later on when the Church included people from many different parts of the Roman empire and not only Jews.

For a study of the gospel tradition an investigation of Jesus' and Early Christianity's relations to the Jewish behavioural tradition is extremely important, especially in the light of Jesus' admonition to put one's confession and insights into practice: "do" the word.[25] Very roughly speaking, the pattern of Jesus' own attitude to the behavioural aspect of the Jewish mother-tradition is that he shows very little interest in halachic minutiae but a very strong interest in the central ethos of the mother-tradition, which may be summarized in formulas such as "the great and first commandment" (Matt 22:38), "the weightiest matters of the law" (Matt 23:23) or in some other way. His own "new teaching" is a radicalization of the central core within the verbal Torah.[26]

The fact that the ethical teaching of Jesus was strongly centred around the basic norms indicates that he focused the interest of his adherents upon these. This also means — and it is important to observe this — that he even made their practical *imitation* of him rather specific. When in love, admiration and veneration they emulated their master, it was natural to pay the greatest attention to that which was a central concern for the master himself and imitate him in such matters, not in various outward details. Thus the imitation of Jesus assumed a profile different from the imitation of rabbis with different specialisations, in spite of the fact that the same socio-psychological mechanisms were at work in both cases.[27]

This we see very clearly in Paul. When he suggests Christ as a model, he never mentions concrete details in Jesus' conduct but always the central principle in his attitude: his self-sacrificing love demonstrated in action. We can certainly say that all of Paul's direct references to Jesus as

---

[25] I am thinking of all texts where the *motif* is present, not only of passages containing the verb ποιεῖν.

[26] See e.g. my book *Ethos* 33—62, 124—26, and cf. H. Braun, *Spätjüdisch-häretischer und frühchristlicher Radikalismus* (BHT 24; 2 vols; Tübingen: Mohr, 1957).

[27] This is my answer to M. Hengel, *Nachfolge und Charisma* (BZNW 34; Berlin: Töpelmann, 1968) 46—79, who paints a sharp contrast between Jesus and the rabbis. In my opinion Hengel overlooks the general socio-psychological mechanisms which operate in both contexts, in spite of all differences.

an ethical model are concrete examples of ἀγάπη. We also see that Paul sometimes puts forward himself and even other prominent representatives of Jesus' ethos as secondary models for imitation. It should be noted that he aims at the true reception of the message from and about Jesus Christ, thus as words and as a practical life accordingly.[28]

So much for the *general* (primarily ethical) behavioural tradition. But some *specific* parts of Early Christianity's behavioural tradition also deserve attention if we want to put the gospel tradition in a realistic historical framework: (1) rites in the context of worship, (2) practices in teaching and other specific forms of verbal transmission, (3) therapeutic activity.

(1) It goes without saying that the forms of Early Christian worship were borrowed from Jewish practice: liturgical praying, recitation and singing, sacred meals and so on. We can call this the "liturgical tradition of behaviour".

(2) Most interesting for the study of the gospel tradition is of course the specific behaviour of verbal communication and transmission, the forms for reading, teaching, exhortation, discussions and so forth, both the genuine Jewish models with their different degrees of "Hellenization" and the subsequent side-influences from different traditions in the Early Christian milieus. This I shall discuss at length shortly.

(3) A third area requiring special attention concerns the therapeutic practices in Early Christianity: healings and exorcisms, carried out in accordance with the example and, perhaps, instructions of Jesus. This seems to have taken different forms: a more charismatic one, handled by individuals with a specific χάρισμα ἰαμάτων (cf. 1 Cor 12:9), and one of a more institutionalized character, handled by specific men in office (cf. Mark 6:7—13, Jak 5:14—15), with possible combinations and intermediate forms. This aspect of the behavioural tradition is of interest because it was programmatic for Jesus and Early Christianity: to the central task belonged not only preaching and teaching but also healing and exorcism.[29] Therefore we must investigate this part of the behavioural tradition and its relation to the gospel tradition.[30] Which

---

[28] On the imitation motif among the rabbis, see *Memory* 181—89; on the motif in the Pauline material, see 292—94 and *Ethos* 72—76, 89—90, 124—26.

[29] See e.g. Mark 1:39, Matt 4:23, 9:35, Luke 4:16—24, 31—37, 40—41, and Mark 3:13—15, Matt 10:1—8, Luke 9:1—2, Acts 3:6, 4:29—30, 5:12—16.

[30] For literature on the miracles of Jesus, see my book *The Mighty Acts of Jesus According to Matthew* (Scripta minora Reg. Soc. Hum. Lit. Lundensis 1978—1979:9; Lund: Gleerup, 1979). On healing as a vital part of Jesus' activity in Israel, see 20—51.

older models did Jesus himself link up with, totally or in part? To what extent was his own practice an object of imitation? To what extent did he give direct instructions? What role did concrete traditions about Jesus' teaching and therapeutic practice — the gospel tradition — play for Early Christianity's practice in this respect? And can we reckon with the possibility that therapeutic practices in the Church after Easter have influenced the gospel tradition?

3.3.4. Verbal tradition

I have not written the foregoing pages without my reasons. In order to emphasize the need for concreteness in our historical reconstruction and interpretation of the transmission of the gospel tradition, I have tried to draw the reader's attention to pertinent mechanisms in Early Christian tradition which must be taken into consideration when working with the concrete Jesus-tradition.

We are now prepared to enter the central area of our subject, Early Christianity's verbal tradition. I will group my observations and reflections under 10 headings.

3.3.4.1. The information in the Lukan prologue

Let me start with some general comments on the prologue to Luke-Acts (Luk 1:1—4). This is the most important item of information which is preserved from the first Christian centuries about the pre-history of the Gospels. The fragments of information in Papias, Irenaeus, Clement, the prologues etc,[31] certainly deserve all the interest they have received. But these notices are not as old as the Lukan prologue and they seem to give a somewhat anachronistic picture of the origin of the Gospels. They hardly reveal any awareness of two important facts: that the Gospels build upon a common oral tradition and that there must also be some kind of *literary* connection between them, in any case between the synoptics. In this material from the Ancient Church we get the picture of an individual teacher who had preached and tought with great authority and then written down his material himself (Matthew, John) or had some follower who committed his teaching to writing (Mark, Luke). I do not think these items of information are freely made up, but they seem to give us a somewhat anachronistic picture.

---

[31] The most important material from the fathers is conveniently brought together in K. Aland, *Synopsis quattuor evangeliorum* (Stuttgart: Würt. Bibelanstalt, 1964) 531—48. See also W. Rordorf, A. Schneider, *Die Entwicklung des Traditionsbegriffs in der Alten Kirche* (Traditio Christiana 5; Bern & Frankfurt a.M.: Lang, 1983).

Let me quote the ancient prologue to Luke's two-volume work (Luke 1:1—4):

> Since many writers have undertaken to compile an orderly account of the events that have come to fulfilment among us, just as the original eyewitnesses and ministers of the word passed them on to us, I too have decided, after tracing everything carefully from the beginning, to put them systematically in writing for you, Theophilus, so that Your Excellency may realize what assurance you have for the instruction you have received.[32]

Seven points should be observed in this brief text.

(1) "Luke" wants to present an orderly account (διήγησις) of the Jesus-event, but he indicates that this attempt is innovative. Like a number of predecessors, he has felt the need and made the attempt to put together the material about Jesus into an organized, synthetic presentation, but the material did not have this form from the beginning.

(2) Luke classifies his material as tradition and indicates that it is insider-tradition, which is there *intra muros ecclesiae.* It is all about "events that have come to fulfilment among us"; the information has "been passed on to us" (παρέδωσαν ἡμῖν). This means that the material has been preserved and exists within the Church.

(3) Luke also mentions the originators of the material. The traditions stem from "the original eyewitnesses (αὐτόπται) and ministers of the word". In the Lukan usage this means the closest followers and disciples of Jesus, first of all the twelve but hardly exclusively.

(4) The originators are not only called "eyewitnesses" but also "ministers of the word" (ὑπηρέται τοῦ λόγου). Thus, they have not only quoted and reported what they had heard and seen but have also been active as ministers of the word as well, which must mean that they have preached, taught and expounded the scriptures and so on. In Acts 6:4 their main activity is called "ministry of the Word" (διακονία τοῦ λόγου).

(5) Luke knows about many earlier attempts to compile an orderly account of the Jesus-event. "Many" (πολλοί) is certainly a conventional exaggeration, but Luke would hardly use this phrase if he was just thinking of one or two *specific* predecessors.

[32] Fitzmyer's translation. On the exegetical problems in Luke 1:1—4, see J.A. Fitzmyer, *The Gospel According to Luke I—IX* (AB 28; New York: Doubleday, 1981) 287—302, and H. Schürmann, *Das Lukasevangelium* (HTKNT 3:1; Freiburg, Basel, Wien: Herder, 1969) 1—17.

29

(6) For his own part Luke had a special purpose when he wrote his Gospel. It is a matter of dispute whether his words about his own carefulness imply criticism of his predecessors. If so, he expresses himself so discreetly that the reader does not notice it without being suspiscious. One thing, however, Luke expresses clearly. He has a special purpose which obviously his predecessors did not have: his ambition is to write history (cf. also 1:5, 2:1—2, 3:1—2). This aim makes him combine two subjects which usually were kept apart: on the one hand the teaching, work and fate of Jesus, and on the other hand the fate of the Christian message during the first decades of the Church.[33] Luke's way of dedicating his work to the illustrious Theophilus gives us reason for believing that his opus is not written for the communities but for cultivated individuals within the Church and presumably also outside it: for the public market.[34] This confers on the Gospel of Luke a *specific* nature which must be kept in mind both in the discussion about Luke's way of handling the oral tradition and in the analysis of the relations between the three synoptic Gospels.[35]

(7) Luke reveals here — as he does in the main text of his work as well — that he has a general respect for reliable tradition and faithful traditionists. I do not think it is correct to interpret this respect as nothing but a secondary feature, due to the point of time, the individuality of the author or his special purpose. This seems to be typical insider-evaluations: respect for "our own" tradition and a preference for "those in the know".

3.3.4.2. Oral and written transmission

Language is a vocal means of communication; it is spoken, it sounds, it is heard. As we are presently dealing with antiquity — thus not the time of the printed word or the time of silent reading — it is important to keep in mind that even the *written* word is a vocal word. It is very misleading if, in our discussions about conditions in antiquity, we put oral and written delivery side by side on the same level as two entirely comparable entities and proclaim that the one is made for the eye, the other for the ear, the one is visual, the other auditive and so on.[36] In antiquity, words were

---

[33] Cf. I.H. Marshall, Luke and his "Gospel", *Das Evangelium und die Evangelien* 289—308.
[34] Cf. M. Dibelius, *Aufsätze zur Apostelgeschichte* (FRLANT 60; 5th ed.; Göttingen: Vandenhoeck & Ruprecht, 1968) 79 and 118.
[35] Cf. W.C. van Unnik, Remarks on the Purpose of Luke's Historical Writing (Luke 1:1—4), *Sparsa collecta* (3 vols.; NovTSup 29—31; Leiden: Brill, 1973) 1. 6—15.
[36] Thus W. H. Kelber, *The Oral and the Written Gospel. The Hermeneutics of Speaking and Writing in the Synoptic Tradition, Mark, Paul, and Q* (Philadelphia: Fortress, 1983) passim.

written down in order to be read out. Even the written word was formulated for the ear. One read aloud when reading for oneself or asked a
slave or a friend to read aloud. (Public reading was also common.) There
is much evidence for this in the sources, both from the Greek-Roman
and from the Jewish worlds. The author *speaks,* and the reader *speaks* as
well; the reader *hears* what the text *says,* even when reading alone, and so
on.[37] Even the copyists used to read vocally when they copied.

This also means that it is misleading to say that the written word is
visual. Before the eye nothing but a picture stands: letters, lines, columns.
The illiterate can see no more than this visual picture. To be able to read
is to be able to change letters and lines into functioning language: otherwise one cannot understand the text. This was especially obvious in the
youth of the art of writing, during the millennia when one read aloud.
The writing down means that the spoken word is frozen in order to be
thawed and revived as language, as a spoken word. Therefore, oral
devices are very self-evident even in written texts: rhythm, metre,
euphony, paronomasia, alliterations and the like. It is a great mistake to
believe that the written word was something totally different from the
spoken word in antiquity. This applies both to the Greek-Roman and to
the Near Eastern cultures.

During recent generations some very interesting research has been
devoted to "orality" in societies where writing has not yet influenced
language. Attempts have been made not least by English and American
scholars to clarify in what way the purely spoken word functions and how
a purely oral tradition is handed on.[38] It is very clear that writing influences the thinking and speaking in the direction of discursiveness and
linearity; it may even influence the experience itself. But pure "orality"
can only be found in a few societies. In "civilized" societies untouched
orality is dead almost everywhere. In societies where writings have been
in use for a long time it is very hard to find source material that is completely uninfluenced by writing. On the other hand, it is of course important to remember that even in our own "developed" societies the oral
language has preserved certain parts of its distinctiveness and has suc-

---

[37] See above all J. Balogh, "Voces paginarum", *Philologus* 82 (1926—27) 84—109,
202—40, and further G.L. Hendrickson, Ancient Reading, *The Classical Journal* 25
(1929—30) 182—96, and E. S. McCartney, Notes on Reading and Praying Audibly,
Classical Philology 43 (1948) 184—87. — On the conditions in the Ancient Near East, see
O. Roller, *Das Formular der paulinischen Briefe. Ein Beitrag zur Lehre vom antiken Briefe*
(BWANT 58; Stuttgart: Kohlhammer, 1933) 220—23; rabbinic material in S. Krauss,
Talmudische Archäologie (3 vols.; Schriften, ed. by Ges. zur Förd. der Wiss. des Judent.;
Leipzig: Fock, 1912) 3.227—29. See also *Memory* 163—68 and cf. n. 82 below.
[38] For literature, see Kelber, *Oral* 227—39.

ceeded in doing so in the face of the written language in a surprisingly tough way.

In his very interesting book *The Oral and the Written Gospel* (1983), Werner Kelber has made a broad attempt to interpret the Early Christian process of tradition with the help of the modern folk-loristic model of "orality". His point of departure is that there is a decisive and consistent difference of principle between orality (oral delivery, always flexible) and textuality (written delivery). In his view proper texts are to be found solely within written tradition. From here they may enter the realm of oral tradition as memorized texts, but that causes no change: now they are borrowed, and if they have a firm wording they are a foreign body in the oral context. Orality is always characterized by flexibility: the speaker adapts his words to his listeners; in one way these influence his speaking so strongly that sender, message and receivers form a synthetic unity: "the oral synthesis".[39] In orality the narrator takes his raw material from an inherited stock-in-trade of words, formulas, motifs, themes, plots, devices etc., but he never formulates his presentation of the "tradition" in exactly the same way twice. Every delivery ("performance") is a new variation; the model is "composition in transmission".[40] Now Kelber tries to demonstrate that the Jesus-tradition started as orality and went through its most decisive alteration when the written word could take full control, i.e. when the oral gospel tradition had become written Gospels. The first written Gospel — Mark — was a revolutionary phenomenon, a radical shift of medium: orality had become textuality, flexibility had become a fixed entity, the audible word had become a visible word, the living speach had become a book.

There are many good observations and stimulating points of view in Kelber's book, and some of them could be illustrated with material from the theological discussions in the Ancient Church and at the Reformation about "the living voice of the gospel" *(viva vox evangelii)*. Yet, Kelber's approach seems to me to be basically inadequate.

The society where Jesus appeared — even the small towns in the Galilean countryside — was no pre-literary society. Nothing indicates that the formative milieu of Jesus was not at all or only to a small degree influenced by the written word. It seems to be quite clear that the holy scriptures were in high regard in the family and synagogue community in which Jesus grew up, and that influences from these writings strongly affected thinking and speaking in this milieu and with Jesus himself. Nor is there any doubt that Jesus had obtained a considerable education in

[39] Kelber 19, 40 (n. 179), 147, 168—77.
[40] Kelber 30 and passim.

reading the holy scriptures — including memorizing of the texts — and was strongly affected by this extensive text material. All the scriptural words, formulas, motifs and patterns as well as allusions and quotations we meet in the recorded sayings of Jesus cannot possibly be secondary altogether.

The verbal Jesus-tradition was at no stage pure "orality" in the meaning folk-lorists give the term. Already in the mind of Jesus the incipient parts of the gospel tradition were influenced by an older tradition which was partly oral, partly written, and the gospel tradition retained in many ways this contact the whole time until the final redaction of the synoptic Gospels, and afterwards as well.

3.3.4.3. The interaction between written and oral tradition

Occasionally, in certain places in his book, Kelber is aware of many complications,[41] but his main reasoning is always based on a view which makes a very clear contrast between the spoken and the written words: "Contemporary theorists of orality appear virtually unanimous in emphasizing the linguistic integrity of the difference between spoken versus written words".[42] When in an "oral society" one version of the ongoing oral narrating is committed to writing, a radical shift of media occurs, and this shift has far-reaching consequences. It seems to me, however, that this model cannot give us much help in trying to understand the relation between oral and written Torah-tradition and gospel tradition in antiquity. The complicated situation can be illustrated with an example.[43] Let us imagine how a text from the written tradition, e.g. from the Book of Isaiah, could function in a synagogue in Galilee in the New Testament period. The inherited message from Isaiah appeared in many different forms:

(1) It appeared in the scroll in the form of letters, lines and columns as כתב (kĕtāb), "the writing", before the eyes, in other words as an orthographic tradition in Hebrew;

(2) It was read aloud in an inherited audible wording, as מקרא (miqrā'), "the reading", a traditional, vocal reading in the old original language;

(3) It was also mediated in a translated form, transposed to the living language of the people (Aramaic) as תרגום (targûm), a tradition of translation. This could be of different kinds but the most common choice

---

[41] Kelber e.g. 17, 23, 29—30, 73—74, 93.

[42] p. 14. Kelber's book contains numerous untenable generalizations of the differences between the oral and the written word.

[43] Cf. Memory 67—70, and 33—42; Riesner, Jesus 137—51.

was a middle way between a too literal and a too free translation. In order to make the ancient text comprehensible, the targumist adapted it (a) to the new language, (b) to a new situation (more or less);

(4) If the reading and the targum was followed by a didactic speach, מדרש, דרשה (*midrāsh, derāshāh*), the content of the text could be clarified in more detail in a fourth form of delivery, as midrashic tradition: exposition and application.

To the extent that the old Isaiah scroll was in the hands of learned men at a synagogue service, it may have happened that the people in the synagogue in New Testament time had the text presented to themselves in a more clear and "living" way than those who listened to it when it was read the first time. This is the case in spite of the fact that the written text had hardly been altered at all during the centuries since the book was written. Radical shift of medium or not — the question is not very simple!

In the synagogue service the problem of oral and written transmission was solved brilliantly; what solution could be more ingenious? The two media stood in very intimate interaction, the advantages of both were exploited and the disadvantages were reduced to a minimum.

I am not saying that the gospel tradition was handed on this way. My example from the Jewish milieu was chosen to show how complicated the relation between oral and written transmission can be; a simple model from oral cultures does not take us very far.

3.3.4.4. *Firm and flexible elements*

There are very clear differences between spontaneous oral talking and a markedly written presentation, and it is very interesting to study them. But a simple distinction between orality and textuality does not solve many problems. Both oral and written delivery and transmission can appear in a thousand forms. Both can be flexible — not only the oral tradition; both can be firm — not only the written tradition. And two of the most fascinating problems here are (1) what role the firm elements play, and (2) the very interaction between these firm elements and the great flexible, "living" part of the verbal tradition.

In spite of forceful criticism of principle, Kelber offers a sympathetic and partly very good picture of my own approach (pp. 8—14), but curiously enough he fails to see the role of the flexible part of tradition and of the interplay between firmness and flexibility in my approach.[44] My starting point was the observation that the ancient Jewish *tradition*

---

[44] See especially *Memory* 19—21, 41—42, 71—78, 79—84.

was so rich, living, flexible, and creative, in most contexts, and yet many *texts* were transmitted with extreme care for the exact wording. Therefore my question was: where and how were texts reproduced without significant change? In other words, I indicated a *total* picture but concentrated my actual attention on a specific *part* of the whole.[45]

It is not true that "texts" only appear in written tradition or in traditions which are influenced by the written word: It is not true that all oral presentation is adapted to the listener and therefore constantly influenced by the situations of use. As for the ideal linguistic communication, it is of course a fact that the speaker's words are perfectly adapted to the listener and his situation, but this only happens when the speaker has an unlimited freedom of choosing his words himself. As soon as he tries to render what somebody else has said — reproduce the real utterance of this person — his possibilities of adapting his language to the listener are reduced. And the more he has reasons for giving a direct *quotation,* the less he can decide what wording his communication shall have. The one who will programmatically hand on verbal tradition has only limited freedom.

It is quite clear that the phenomenon we call a "text" — a self-contained, rounded utterance, shorter or longer, with a more or less fixed wording — has arisen in the *oral* stage of language. We may take the proverb as an example. It is a text which has a very firm wording indeed; even a very slight alteration brings about protests from the audience! And the proverb is clearly an *oral* text. There are written collections, but they are secondary. There are proverbs formulated by some writer, but they are imitations. We also know of other oral texts with a very firm wording: certain types of songs and poems, certain sacred texts, legal texts, genealogies and so forth. Not least interesting are those texts that are often handed on in spite of the fact that the transmitter himself does not understand the words he is reciting from memory.[46]

Therefore it seems to me that we cannot possibly accept the simplified view that oral communication is always a flexible communication, the firmest elements of which are certain standardized expressions and formulas and other clichés, motifs, plots, certain linguistic devices and the like. And it is quite clear that we do not get very helpful models from this type of orality for our study of Early Christianity and its mother-tradition in antiquity.

On the other hand, it is extremely important to investigate the *interaction* between the fixed and the flexible elements in tradition, especially

[45] *Memory* 19—32, 33—42, 71—78.
[46] *Memory* 123—36.

the model "text and commentary". This applies to different types of oral tradition and different individual texts with an oral pre-history. But it also applies to written tradition. Written texts were often changed in antiquity, a little in any case, but more important is the fact that they were transformed into an oral presentation when they were read and thereby usually got support from additional, flexible oral language. As long as written documents were hardly more than an aid to the oral presentation, the declamations and readings were connected with clarifying oral elements. When anyone in antiquity read a book aloud for others, the reader or some other expert had to be prepared for questions: the obscurities of the text were to be mastered by re-reading, clarifications, comments and perhaps exposition.[47] Our own perfectly printed book-pages cause us to miss historical realities of this kind.

Kelber's main interest is not history but rather language and literary phenomena.[48] I do not find much about the behavioural, institutional and material dimensions of tradition in his approach. In fact his model "orality contra textuality" does not seem to harmonize very well with the historical realities we get a glimpse of in our sources. In the New Testament Jesus from Nazareth is nowhere presented as a popular "performer" who entertains crowds with oral narratives or oral poetry of the type folk-lorists often speak of. He has original traits but he is classified as a teacher and a prophet ($\delta\iota\delta\acute{\alpha}\sigma\varkappa\alpha\lambda\circ\varsigma$, $\pi\rho\circ\varphi\acute{\eta}\tau\eta\varsigma$) — and more than a teacher and a prophet (cf. below 3.3.4.7).[49] It is said that he preaches and teaches ($\varkappa\eta\rho\acute{\upsilon}\sigma\sigma\epsilon\iota\nu$, $\delta\iota\delta\acute{\alpha}\sigma\varkappa\epsilon\iota\nu$) and that he heals sick people and expels demons. It seems very odd to me to put Jesus in the category where the folk-lorists place their oral narrators and oral poets.

Our sources also tell us that Jesus used to teach with the aid of $\pi\alpha\rho\alpha\beta\circ\lambda\alpha\acute{\iota}$ (משלים).[50] In the ancient Jewish texts we see that משל (māshāl) is a very broad designation which can be used for a long series of different linguistic creations. But these have three things in common: (1) they are texts — not free streams of words, (2) they are brief — not whole books, and (3) they have an artistic design — they differ from bland everyday speech.

---

[47] Even the classical procedure of the grammarian, who taught children to read texts, is revealing. It included four elements: criticism of the text ($\delta\iota\acute{\circ}\rho\vartheta\omega\sigma\iota\varsigma$), reading ($\grave{\alpha}\nu\acute{\alpha}\gamma\nu\omega-\sigma\iota\varsigma$), explication ($\grave{\epsilon}\xi\acute{\eta}\gamma\eta\sigma\iota\varsigma$) and judgement ($\varkappa\rho\acute{\iota}\sigma\iota\varsigma$): *Memory* 124—25.

[48] *Oral* 18; cf. 8 and 70—77.

[49] See further Riesner, *Jesus,* and cf. now E.P. Sanders, *Jesus and Judaism* (London: SCM, 1985).

[50] esp. Mark 4:2, 33—34, Matt 13:3, 34—35.

Related to Jesus' custom of teaching with the aid of parabolai (let me call them meshalim, in the plural) is the fact that all items of the proper sayings-tradition from Jesus extant in the synoptic Gospels, have the form of meshalim: the items are texts, they are brief, and they are artistically designed. This applies to the extremely short items (let me call them logia) and to the somewhat longer but still very short narrative parables. One can always discuss how to divide the "speaches" of Jesus in the synoptic Gospels, but let us disregard differences in detail for the moment. In his book *Jesus als Lehrer* (1981), Rainer Riesner divides the synoptic collections of sayings into 247 independent units. About 65% of these are not more than two verses long. Only 12% are longer than four verses.[51]

The possibility that this picture only reflects a late stage of transmission, when writtenness and textuality had got control over a tradition which was oral and flexible in its first stage, seems to be quite unrealistic. There were firm elements within the synoptic word-tradition even from the beginning; a mashal is a mashal.

On the other hand, there was of course also a living, flexible exchange of words. The sources show not only that Jesus communicated meshalim but also that he was talking to people, answering questions, discussing, preaching, teaching, exhorting etc. All this was of course not done exclusively in the form of meshalim.

We have observed the fact that the firm text often needs commentary. This applies to texts of the mashal-type to a special degree. When in the Gospels we see that Jesus must explain what he has said in a mashal, this may not be a secondary feature in the tradition. Nobody can express puzzling proverbs and enigmatic parables without being questioned or feeling himself that something needs explanation. Meshalim — most types of this complex category — evoke curiosity, wonder, pondering, questions, discussions.[52]

As for the *narratives* about Jesus, a few exceptions may lead one to think of oral narration of the common popular type (flexible "composition in transmission"). Martin Dibelius called these narratives *Novellen* (Tales) and regarded them as more "secular" (weltlich) than the other material and more secondary as well. He also thought that these narratives had not been in use in Early Christian preaching as had the other narratives

[51] Riesner, *Jesus* 392—93.
[52] From this point of view note e.g. Mark 4:10, 34, 7:17, 8:16—17, 9:32, 10:10, 24, 26, 13:14.

but that they stemmed from special "narrators".[53] On this point Dibelius has received very little following. Kelber now puts forward the thesis that the pre-Markan narrative material in its entirety comes from oral narration of the common popular type.

A thorough analysis of the entire narrative material in the synoptic tradition will reveal to what extent a thesis of this kind can stand the test. But I do not think this model is very adequate as to narrative tradition either. Our sources from Early Christianity do not say a word about narrators of this type. And what we meet in the bulk of the synoptic narrative tradition is texts which very briefly and schematically present single episodes from the activity of Jesus. The presentation is usually so concentrated and terse that the wording does not allow much scope for variations. We read a brief description of the situation leading up to a saying of Jesus, a recording of a conversation with one or two rejoinders, or a brief account of a case of healing or exorcism. The superfluous words in a pericope of this kind are few, the margin for variations very small. It is difficult to see it otherwise than that these condensed narratives have been *texts* even at their oral stage, notwithstanding that the demand for unaltered wording has not been as strong in the narrative elements as in the sayings of Jesus in these texts. It is also easy to imagine that the *narrative* texts have been more readily influenced by the narrator's overall picture of Jesus and of his actual aim than are the sayings of Jesus.[54]

In his book, Werner Kelber stresses the importance of considering the social involvement of the gospel tradition (pp. 14—43 et passim). To him, however, the social factors occur primarily in the form of social pressure from the audience on the narrator. The presence and character of the audience, and the social surroundings of it, influence rather strongly the way the narrator formulates his presentation. Kelber characterizes my approach as "a model of passive transmission" and notes in *my* description "a virtual exemption of the oral Torah from active social engagement" (pp. 8—14). This is a misunderstanding. My view is that the Torah was a very "living" factor in the Jewish milieu and that the gospel tradition belonged to the concrete existence of the Jesus-movement and the Early Church, and was transmitted within the frame of the Early Christian "work with the word".[55] In *Memory and Manuscript* I attempted to give a concrete picture of some aspects of this "work with the word",

---

[53] *Die Formgeschichte des Evangeliums* (2nd ed.; Tübingen: Mohr, 1933) 66—100, esp. 66—67, 94—100.

[54] Cf. my article *Weg* 96—101.

[55] *Memory* 324—35, *Tradition* 37—47, *Origins* 67—91, and *Weg* passim.

which, of course, was influenced by the social conditions of the teachers involved. Their way of collecting, selecting, formulating and re-formulating, interpreting and expounding, grouping and re-grouping the traditional texts does not go on without influence from their present situation: they are affected themselves, they take positions themselves, they get questions from others and so on. — Not even the most "academic" halachists among *the Rabbis* were completely uninfluenced by the social life around them; such is the case even more so far as the "haggadic" teachers are concerned!

3.3.4.5. The origin and character of the gospel tradition

If Jesus was a child prodigy and if he was remarkable when growing up, it is possible that his family spread a sort of tradition about him already at that time, in free wording. But we can only speculate about this; in the Gospels the material from the time before Jesus began his public ministry is both scanty and fragile. The proper, specific Early Christian tradition does not start until Jesus "appears publicly before Israel".

A. How can we imagine the beginning of the gospel tradition which records Jesus' preaching and teaching in *words*?

It starts when Jesus "opens his mouth and teaches" and gains sympathizers, adherents, and disciples, who accept his message.

We have already underlined two basic facts: that our sources tell us that Jesus taught with the aid of short, artistically formulated texts, and that the extant material in the synoptic sayings tradition is a series of such texts. It is important to notice that the synoptics use the same word for parables and logia: both are parabolai (meshalim).[56] We must of course analyse the material more closely and categorize it more precisely for our aims, but it is interesting that the Early Christian transmitters and evangelists did not see any difference in principle between logia and parables. Evidently they were transmitted in the same way, even if it was easier to make adjustments in the wordings of a longer parable than in a brief proverbial logion.

These texts were presumably transmitted as memorized texts in roughly the same way as the Jewish mashal-tradition, with roughly the same technique as Jewish material of similar types (note that the haggadic material had somewhat freer wording than the halacha-rules). I

---

[56] Note how the word $\pi\alpha\varrho\alpha\beta o\lambda\acute{\eta}$ is used in most cases in the parable chapter (Mark 4:1—34, Matt 13:1—52, Luke 8:4—18), and cf. Mark 7:17, Matt 15:15, Luke 6:39. In Luke 4:23 the word means "proverb".

have tried to illustrate this in my previous writings on the subject,[57] and need not repeat myself here.

I have also stressed the fact that all verbal tradition has a very wide sector of flexible words. This phenomenon is not, however, as interesting as are the firm elements, since it is so general, so common, and so difficult to separate from everyday talking. But it is important to be aware of the fact that the verbal tradition does include this phenomenon and that it is a vital part of it: *texts* must very often be interpreted or expounded, especially if they have the form of puzzling logia or riddlesome parables.[58]

I do not think I shall linger on this for the moment. But let me illustrate the phenomenon that the verbal tradition includes an interaction between elements of different character with an example I drew attention to in *Memory and Manuscript* (p. 145). In the parable chapter of Matthew (13:1—52) we find Jesus teaching with the aid of parables. In order to illuminate the different ways of receiving the message of the Reign of Heaven Jesus relates to the people (1) the parable of the sower (vv. 3—9). This is a text with a firm wording; the small margin of alteration can be measured by way of a comparison between the parallels. The content of the parable is also clarified (2) in the form of an interpretative exposition presented as complementary teaching for the disciples (vv. 10—23). The vocabulary is of another type in this exposition than in the parable itself, and many signs give us reason to think that these wordings were less fixed at the beginning than were the wordings of the parable itself. In the long run, however, they have become fixed as well. The parable is finally (3) treated as a well-known text with a name: ἡ παραβολὴ τοῦ σπείραντος (v. 18). For the stranger this name is an empty designation. But within

---

[57] In *Memory* I worked on the base of a very broad conception of the word "Torah". I did not take it in the narrow sense "law" but in its broadest meaning, as a collective designation for the Jew's sacred authoritative tradition in its entirety (cf. above n. 12). I also stressed the well-known fact that, within this circle, the haggadic material had normally a freer wording than the halacha-rules, and the fact that "most of the gospel material is haggadic material", 335 (with reference to 96—97 and 146—48); see also 136—45, 177—81 and further *Tradition* 33—37, *Origins* 67—77, *Weg* 93—96. Yet many critics have ascribed to me the view that Jesus was a Torah-teacher in the meaning a "teacher of the law". When I say that Jesus was a "parabolist" (מרשל, *mōshēl*) I only specify more precisely the designation "haggadist" (cf. *Origins* 70). Kelber (*Oral* 38, n. 131) is mistaken when he takes this as a revocation of my earlier position (that Jesus was a "teacher of the law"!).

[58] See above, nn. 12 and 44.

40

the circle where this parable is a well-known text from Jesus, this name is a terse actualization of the parable and its message.[59]

Here we get a concrete example of the inner secrets of the verbal tradition. Explicit and implicit forms, exhaustive and concise versions may lie side by side. A wealth of different forms is natural in a milieu where a certain verbal tradition is cultivated. One can quote a text verbally, or almost verbally, one can render it more freely, paraphrase it or hand on its message in the form of an interpretation; one can condense it into a brief formula, even a name.[60] If we come across one of these forms we cannot conclude that the other firms did not exist for this author. To ask how much Paul knew of the concrete Jesus-tradition — or in what forms he knew it — is not the same as studying direct quotations in the letters he occasionally wrote to particular communities.[61]

B. As for *the mighty deeds* of Jesus, the rumours certainly spread as soon as somebody was impressed by Jesus. But the inner circle within the Jesus-movement and the Church afterwards claimed to have more definite knowledge. During the time of Jesus there perhaps was no urgent reason for creating firm texts about the mighty acts of the master. Possibly, however, some such texts were needed when Jesus sent out his disciples in order to spread his message during his activity in Galilea; the traditions about this commissioning do not seem to be post-Easter fictions.[62] In Matt 11:4—6 par., we get an interesting picture of a situation in which some of John the Baptist's disciples are made transmitters of Jesus-tradition to the Baptist. What occasional "Jesus-propagandists" said about the master (cf. e.g. Mark 1:45, 5:19—20) is not easy to know; their narration was hardly of the concise synoptic type.[63]

On the whole, I think we must conclude that the real need for brief, pointed narratives about the characteristic deeds of Jesus did not arise until after the departure of the master, when the leadership shifted over from Jesus himself to others, above all the twelve. When they preached

---

[59] Another example is the parable of the tares in Matt 13: mashal (24—30), exposition (37—43), name (36); *Memory* 145. We must also remember that pupils in the Hellenistic schools learned both to present a theme briefly and to develop it broadly (*brevitas, amplificatio*).

[60] See further *Memory* 130—36, 171—81.

[61] *Memory* 290—302, *Origins* 33—41. Cf. T. Holtz, Jesus-Überlieferung und Briefliteratur, *Wiss. Z. Univ. Halle* 34'85 G, H. 1 (1984) 103—12.

[62] E.E. Ellis, New Directions in Form Chriticism, *Jesus Christus in Historie und Theologie* (Festschrift H. Conzelmann; Tübingen: Mohr, 1975) 299—315, 302—04.

[63] Note, however, Riesner, *Jesus* 487—88.

and taught about Jesus as the Messiah, the Son of God, and discussed his secrets with each other and with opponents and critics, it certainly was not natural to confine themselves to the sayings of Jesus. And when they scrutinized the holy scriptures in order to understand the Jesus-events better and find prohetical hints about him, it was maybe near at hand to formulate brief texts about his most typical deeds and about other important episodes in his life on earth. Even these brief narrative texts were probably transmitted by way of memorization; *the primordial sayings-tradition set the pattern.*

C. *The passion narrative* has certainly had a specific position from a very early time. In this case the events themselves were coherent; the moments came in rapid succession, not as isolated episodes, and the event as a whole cried out for another explanation than the official one that the authorities had silenced a deceiver ($\pi\lambda\acute{\alpha}\nu os$). Here the adherents of Jesus needed an interpretation "from within" to set up against the official declarations of the outsiders. It is interesting to see that the passion narrative is a necklace of episodes but that these — or most of them — belong intimately together, because they narrate and interpret a common chain of events.[64]

As for this decisive part of the Jesus-tradition, the New Testament books are full of verbal presentations in the most different forms, from brief condensed formulas to extensive expositions in free words (the speeches in Acts, the letters).

3.3.4.6. *The production of texts: creation, reshaping, compilation*

In the New Testament discipline we must often tackle problems which initially seem to be unsolvable but which eventually turn out to be possible to handle. Let me now mention a set of such questions.

The form critics increased our sensitivity to the *forms* of the gospel material. Since then the achievements of redaction critics, composition critics and text theorists of various schools have sharpened our sensitivity still more and given us even better instruments for discerning the form and anatomy of the synoptic texts. At present, text pragmatic studies

---

[64] This ancient insight, stressed by the three pioneer form critics, has been strongly radicalized by R. Pesch in his commentary on the Gospel of Mark and in his book *Das Evangelium der Urgemeinde. Wiederhergestellt und erläutert von Rudolf Pesch* (Freiburg i.B.: Herder, 1979). See also Pesch's impressive response to his critics, Das Evangelium in Jerusalem, *Das Evangelium und die Evangelien* 113—55.

seem to be à la mode: one brings the intended addressees of the texts into focus and treats the texts as means of communication.

I think, however, that we can ameliorate these analyses somewhat even by working more concretely than we usually do with some elementary *historical* questions concerning the very making of the New Testament texts: How did Jesus and Early Christianity proceed, technically speaking, when they formulated and reformulated their texts? In my opinion we need rather concrete ideas of the very process of creation, both concerning the individual texts and the text collections, the final written Gospels included.

Generally speaking, I think we can isolate the *creation* of a text from its various uses, and fix the process of creation as an act in itself. We know that a text can arise suddenly through the prompting of the moment, in practical situations of various kind, but even then it is reasonable to ask how this came about. In most cases, however, the text is created outside the practical situations wherein it will be used, and the author is well aware of what happens in the process.[65] This applies especially to written texts.

Studies in the psychology of artistic inspiration[66] show that different authors give different answers to the question of how they create their texts. Some of them claim just to "receive" texts under strong inspiration; the poems "come" to them completed and perfect with metre, rhythm, rhyme and everything, and need only to be written down. Others say that their texts, even those which give the impression of being strongly "inspired", are the result of hard intellectual labour. Yet others declare that the texts certainly come to them in moments of inspiration but that they must be revised very thoroughly nevertheless in order to stand. Of course there are many possibilities between the extremes here.

Now to our material. I cannot discuss every category of text and all stages. Let me confine myself to three levels and to the main types of synoptic texts.

A. *Text creation.* (1) How did the genuine *sayings* of Jesus originate? Was Jesus a man of strong inspiration, who just "received" his logia and parables? Or was he a man who created them very consciously? In the latter case, did he normally do so in contexts of conversation, teaching, extemporaneous preaching or other communal contexts? Or did he do it in

---

[65] *Weg* 85—91, 96—101.
[66] T. Andræ, *Mystikens psykologi. Besatthet och inspiration* (2nd ed.; Stockholm: Verbum, 1968) 176—444.

solitude? Did he repeat his texts in order to implant them firmly in his own memory? And what role did the disciples play? Were they, as it were, his note-books? Questions of this kind may seem totally impossible now, and some of them may even sound ridiculous, but they may become possible to deal with once we have tried to come to grips with the process of text creation.[67]

(2) How did the *episodal narratives* of Jesus originate? In this case it is hardly realistic to think of a markedly inspirational process of creation. Early Christian prophets did not present such texts. They were certainly formulated very consciously. How? Did it take place in a situation of teaching or discussion, so that someone in the session had the task of formulating the text while the others listened to his presentation and contributed with proposals of amelioration until the text was finished and accepted? Or were there always specific, skilful individuals responsible for such texts; men who created them individually outside the proper situations of teaching or study? How did that occur, to be precise? Were specific patterns consciously followed? Old Testament patterns, contemporary Jewish patterns, more decidedly Hellenistic patterns, from various schools? Was the form of the text chosen with special regard to its *primary* use, that which the form critics call its proper Sitz im Leben?[68] To what extent were notebooks used in this situation (the Rabbinic material shows that such tools were not *necessary*)? The questions may be multiplied.

(3) Does the distinctiveness of the *passion narrative* motivate the supposition that it was created in some other way than the rest of the narrative traditions? In that case, how? Most of the episodes in the passion narrative are, as we know, self-contained units but at the same time natural links within the story at large: was this a result of conscious considerations on the part of those who formulated the passion narrative? Were more or different people involved in the creation of this narrative than in the other cases? Was it written down earlier than the episodal stories, maybe even from the start? (It could mainly function as a memorized text, to be recited from memory just the same.)

[67] I have collected some concrete material for comparison in *Memory* esp. 130—36, 171—89. I also think that the present interest in the devices of ancient rhetoric will provide us with assistance in this connection. See, e.g., V.K. Robbins, *Jesus the Teacher. A Socio-Rhetorical Interpretation of Mark* (Philadelphia: Fortress, 1984).

[68] For my part I do not think the text was actually *formulated* in the situation for which it was primarily intended to be *used; Weg* 85—91, 96—98.

B. *Reshaping of texts.* As for the transmission of the fixed texts, the methods of the transmitter and the receiver, I think I shall not repeat here what I have written in other connections. But a cluster of questions could be formulated concerning the deliberate reformulations of the firm texts during the phase of transmission. In *Memory and Manuscript*[69] I offer some hints about the way in which transmitted texts were altered in the Rabbinic schools and sessions, but I wish I had written more about that; it would have prevented the misunderstanding that the Rabbis never changed their texts or that all types of Rabbinic texts had the same firm wording. Here, a good deal of work remains to be done if we want to understand how the variations in the firm texts have arisen.[70]

C. *Text compilation.* At the stage of the creation of the large written Gospels we have to ask how the Gospels were produced, technically speaking. How do we imagine that Mark, Matthew, Luke, John — let me call them so — actually proceeded, when they produced their famous books? Who were these men and how well were they versed in the Early Christian tradition in its entirety? How well were they socialized in Early Christianity's behavioural tradition, ethically, didactically, liturgically? What position did they have in the Church seen as a kind of institution? (Did each of them, when writing his book, have the authority of a great apostle behind himself?) And how did this influence their writing? How familiar were they with the broad verbal tradition of the Church? How much did they know of the oral textual tradition? How much did they have in the form of documents? How did they collect their material? Did they travel, search for collections, consult informants? And how did they actually proceed when compiling their books? Did they have the scrolls and codices before themselves? Did they know them more or less by heart? Did they feel a duty to copy visually from the columns in the *Vorlagen* or could they follow some freer model and adapt their texts in a more targumic way? Did they have in their memory oral versions of the pericopes present in their written sources, and, in such cases, did these versions have the same authority for them as the written versions? Did they use loose notes for the first phase of their attempts to combine their sources? Did they rewrite their drafts many times? Etc., etc. Such questions are not unrealistic; I think we should try to find answers, in any case

[69] e.g. 77—78, 97—98, 103—12, 120—21, 152—53. Cf. also *Tradition* 37—40.

[70] J. Neusner has now summarized his illuminating studies of the specific Rabbinic methods of transmitting abbreviated halacha-rules (apodoses) in the Mishna, in a recent book, *The Memorized Torah: The Mnemonic System of the Mischnah* (Brown Judaic Studies 96; Chico: Scholars, 1985).

for our own silent use. If we cannot form a concrete conception of the process of compiling the Gospels we have reasons to surmise that something is wrong with our solution of the synoptic question and of many other related topics.

Furthermore, if we come to grips with concrete questions of this kind, perhaps we can then also formulate criteria for deciding whether a text has been created — or reworked — as an *oral* text or if it has been produced in *written* form. I do not think we have any proper criteria for this so far.

3.3.4.7. The synthetization of the text material

According to Rudolf Bultmann,[71] the individual elements of the gospel tradition originated first, independently of each other, but it was "in the nature of the case" that they were gathered in collections which gradually became more extensive and finally were written down. The synoptic evangelists were collectors and editors rather than authors. Yet, Mark made a pioneer achievement when writing his Gospel as the first in the series. Here the loosely conglomerated material was interpreted and organized along main lines taken from the Christology and the kerygma of the Hellenistic Church.

Kelber (pp. 44—89 and passim) objects that nothing in orality makes writing natural. The narration about Jesus in Early Christianity was by nature oral, pluriform and multidirectional. When Mark changed the flourishing tradition into a linear account and wrote it down, new factors were decisive, in part pronouncedly anti-traditional factors (pp. 184—226).

I do not think we can get a realistic picture of the synthetizing process if we do not consider all the dimensions of the Early Christian tradition.

This tradition was intra-ecclesiastical. The evangelists were hardly very impressed by pluriform outsider-rumours and multi-directional talk about Jesus among the people. But they were certainly very well acquainted with the insider-tradition about him. In the communities which arose around the message about Jesus Christ, there was a new, enthusiastic belief in Jesus and a living interest in his person, spirit and will. Here was an "inner tradition", a spiritual atmosphere which repelled negative interpretations of Jesus and cultivated positive ones. Certainly, opinions were divided in some questions and various conflicts were unavoidable, but all who got the floor had a positive overall picture

---

[71] *Die Geschichte der synoptischen Tradition* (FRLANT 29; 2nd ed.; Göttingen: Vandenhoeck & Ruprecht, 1931) 393—400.

of Jesus, his person, spirit and will, and at least a rough idea about his career and fate on earth. Already in the inner tradition there was a certain unity: an attitude towards Jesus which kept that which was said about him within a certain framework and gave it something of an organic unity.

To say this is to draw attention to the effects of "the institutional tradition" at the same time. Institutionalization had shown itself therein that a borderline had arisen between insiders and outsiders, impeding the inflow of wild, foreign or negative interpretations of Jesus. And as for the situation *intra muros:* those who had the highest reputation as experts concerning what Jesus had said and done — especially those who could say that they had heard and seen themselves — certainly had the best chances to set the note as traditionists (cf. e.g. Acts 1, Gal 1—2, 1 John 1:1—4). This reduced the pluralism of the traditions about Jesus.

Even the programmatic "behavioural tradition" which was cultivated within the Church was a synthetizing factor: a foreign body could hardly be tolerated. I am thinking of the "imitation of Christ" as a programmatic model for the Christian's lifestyle but also of the liturgical, didactic, therapeutic and exorcistic activity within the Church. Here we have another unifying factor.

Turning to "the verbal tradition" one must remember that it not only contained a number of isolated quotations from Jesus and episodal narratives about him. There were also unifying elements in this connection. Even the general usage of language in Early Christianity — the flexible, variegated way of speaking about Jesus — formed very soon a certain vocabulary, formulas, motifs, etc., which became typical. These observations remind us that the synthetization of the gospel was not something entirely secondary. *Intra muros* the Jesus-tradition was in *certain* respects always something of a unity, stamped by the same deeply devotional attitude to Jesus. Thus, we are moving *within a frame of unity* when we pose the question of how the very texts about Jesus were synthetized into orderly accounts ($\delta\iota\eta\gamma\dot{\eta}\sigma\epsilon\iota\varsigma$) and became written Gospels.

The transmitted texts contained elements which were summaries and thus paved the way for a natural organization of the concrete texts. I am thinking of verbal elements which either classify and characterize the person of Jesus or briefly summarize and categorize his "works". In the former case I aim at such designations as (Our) teacher, the Prophet, Messiah/Christ, God's Son, the Lord, and the like. These titles characterized the person of Jesus and did so *together;* we know of no early Christian group which could classify Jesus with the aid of only one existing title. In this way a complex but coherent picture of Jesus' person was built up. In Early Christianity all these designations have two things in common: they all characterize *Jesus of Nazareth* and do so in a positive and majestic way. Low or negative designations are not accepted. In the long run, these intra-ecclesiastical titles of Jesus become synonymous; they all function to denote the "whole" Jesus. This is a telling example of their synthetizing and unifying character. — The concrete Jesus-tradition deals almost solely with the man who receives these titles.[72]

In the latter case I have in mind the fact that it was impossible already at the beginning to be content with only individual, episodal narratives about the activity of Jesus. Even from the first moment one had sometimes to be brief. Already when Jesus had preached and taught a couple of times, the disciples and others must have been able to say briefly that Jesus "preached and taught". After a while they could certainly claim that he "preached and taught about the Reign of God". In the same way they must have been able to state in general words, after having seen a couple of mighty acts, that Jesus "cured sick people and expelled demons". Such verbal elements are *unavoidable* in every linguistically developed milieu. We may have different opinions about the factual summaries to be fond in the synoptic Gospels, whether in their present form they are formulated by the evangelist or not. But it would be foolish to think that there was no need for summarizing items of this kind before the written organization of the material.

In this way we can analyse the various parts of the text tradition and observe how the different elements contain items which could help anyone who wanted to organize the material into an orderly account to find a basis for his arrangement. Let me mention a few more examples. Some traditions contained certain geographic or temporal information. Rightly or wrongly, these could offer complementary knowledge for dating or localizing other traditions lacking such information. Of great interest are retrospective or forward-pointing elements, for instance Jesus' words about his mighty deeds (Matt 11:20—24 par.) or his predictions about the passion and resurrection (Mark 8:31 with all the parallels). Elements of this kind facilitate synthesis and organization of the material. Traditions about a conflict between Jesus and his opponents included a natural relationship to the final intervention against him. And the passion narrative made it natural to look for reasons for this

[72] On Jesus as "the only teacher", see *Memory* 332—33, *Tradition* 40—43, *Origins* 47—49, and *Weg* 79—82, 91—93.

condemnation and for evidence for the innocence of Jesus as well in the traditions about his prior teaching and mighty deeds.[73]

I mentioned *the passion narrative.* It has undoubtedly played an eminent role as a first step toward a synthetic, "complete" Gospel. Here, an important part of the history of Jesus was narrated rather early in the form of an orderly account. It is easy to understand that this coherent presentation of the *decisive* part of Jesus' work called for a substructure, a complementary introduction. Martin Kähler's well-known description of the Gospel of Mark as a "passion narrative with an extended introduction" indicates how the evangelist got his most impressive idea for the disposition of his composition.

I break off here. My contention is that a coherent account of "all that Jesus began to do and teach" did not exist at the beginning of Early Christianity and that the first one who wrote a Gospel (I think it was Mark) certainly was a pioneer; yet, *his achievement was hardly very creative.* He had good text material, he did not need to reinterpret it very much, nor change its form very much; even the disposition of the material was near at hand. His achievement was that he actually did what many others could also have done, but that he did it so connaturally with the material that his followers had no reason for constructing a disposition of quite another type.

3.3.4.8. *The process of writing down*

I have already pointed out that the concrete Jesus-tradition arose in a milieu strongly influenced by the holy scriptures; these "were living" through actual reading, translation, interpretation and application. During the whole time from Jesus to the evangelists, the gospel tradition had natural connections with a verbal mother-tradition within which the written word played an important role.

On the other hand, it is very striking that Jesus himself did not write. He was a man who spoke. He talked to people, he preached orally, taught orally, made mighty acts with his oral word etc. Only in one place do our sources mention that he wrote something (John 7:53—8:11), but that was on the ground and nobody knows what it was. Nothing indicates that Jesus wrote down one single logion, parable or speech. Nor is it indicated anywhere that he incited cooperators or disciples to write or that he dic-

---

[73] It is however very interesting to note that the opposition against Jesus' bold way of forgiving sins (Matt 9:1—8 pp.), exorcisms (Matt 9:32—34 and 12:22—24 pp.) and healings on the sabbath (e.g. Matt 12:9—14 pp.) has not been taken into account explicitly in the passion narrative in spite of the fact that all three of these points *could* be classified as capital crimes (a more lenient interpretation was of course also possible).

tated to them. The verbal tradition that Jesus himself initiated, was *oral*.

As for the disciples, it is nowhere mentioned that they took notes or carried notebooks. They "are with" Jesus, they "follow" him, they are his "disciples", they "hear and see", they recollect, and they sometimes question Jesus about something he had said or done. Thus the disciples have seen and heard, they remember, ponder and discuss Jesus and his words and deeds.

When the exclusive master suddenly has departed, the Jesus-movement must be reconstructed and consolidated, a process the sociological consequences of which we can guess only to a certain degree. Nothing indicates, however, that the adherents of Jesus immediately change the medium of communication. They do not sit down in order to write a monograph about Jesus, a book to be duplicated and distributed. They do what we may expect disciples in this milieu to do: they continue in the footsteps of their master, they follow his aims, his behaviour and teaching and perhaps even direct instructions given; they carry on his work along his characteristic lines. What Acts and other New Testament writings say or reflect seems to be very probably true, namely, that the disciples of Jesus preach and teach "in the name of Jesus" and about Jesus, they heal sick people and expel demons "in the name of Jesus" etc.[74] This is not strange at all, especially if earlier they had had the task of helping the master in his work. That the new situation forces them to ponder and discuss more seriously than before the person and work of Jesus, especially his death, goes without saying; that they have much stronger reasons now than before for scrutinizing the holy scriptures in order to gain clarity, is easy to imagine. Of course nothing hampers them from taking various new steps as well; not least their strong conviction that the crucified Jesus is risen and that the Spirit is with them inspires them to new initiatives.

We do not get many indications about the role of writing in this connection. It is possible that notes and notebooks were taken into use early at this time; our sources are, alas, completely silent about it. Even less do we find anywhere an exhortation to use such means. We might, however, imagine that some such writing was done quite informally, for practical reasons; in such case it is no mystery that our sources do not mention it. But it is not at all self-evident. Even less is it true that Early Christianity relied upon the written word.[75] If we look at the words and expressions

---

[74] See e.g. Acts 4:17, 18, 5:28, 40, 9:27, 28, and 3:6, 4:7, 10, 30, 16:18.
[75] Thus Neusner, *Rabbinic Traditions* 3. 154. The gospel tradition was after all not written down immediately, and Paul could not possibly regard his oral teaching as less important or reliable than his letters.

used to characterize the verbal activity of Jesus and Early Christianity, they do not exclude written means but neither do any of them give a clear or even natural hint at the use of written notes which were read aloud. Such words as κηρύσσειν, διδάσκειν, ὁμιλεῖν, διαλέγεσθαι, παρα-καλεῖν, νουθετεῖν κτλ. aim primarily at an oral activity, not at a written one.

However, it can hardly be doubted that notebooks began to be used when the collections became more extensive than in the earliest period. But suddenly, and within a short period of time, from late sixties onwards, written Gospels appeared within the Church. We do not know how many they were, only that four of them very easily forced out the other ones. It is rather difficult to explain this transition to written Gospels. Probably many factors were intertwined and none of them alone was decisive.

We have to do with two questions: Why was the text material gathered into extensive collections? And why were these collections now properly *written down?*

The first question is not difficult to answer. What we call "collecting mania" is a hypertrophy of a general human proclivity: what we find interesting and important we save and gather, be it stamps, anecdotes, knowledge or whatever. It is not difficult to understand that those in Early Christianity who had to use the concrete Jesus-traditions more than others, "collected" such texts; both interest and necessity forced them to do so. It was natural as well that structured collections of this kind emerged and expanded. Even the will to remember leads us to a conscious gathering and grouping of memory material. It is a precaution against forgetfulness. Other factors contributed as well, not least, the needs of the communities. It is easy to imagine that notebooks were more and more taken into use in this work with the texts. Great synthetical collections of the same type as the Q-collection or the Gospel of Mark are thus "in the nature of the case". And proper books had to come, sooner or later.

The Q-collection hardly had as well a structured disposition as did the Gospel of Mark. This Gospel is not merely an extensive notebook (ὑπόμνημα). The author shows a desire to write for others, and his desire has taken him a step further than to the collection of material in a big notebook; he has arranged his texts in accordance with an overall view of Jesus and his work. On the other hand, the Gospel of Mark may not be a proper book (ἔκδοσις) in all respects, written for common use.[76] The

---

[76] On the differences between properly published books and written notes, see V. Burr, Editionstechnik, *RAC* 4 (1959) 597—610. For Jewish material, cf. S. Lieberman,

Gospel of Matthew, for its part, is a book in the more strict sense of the word, even if it was not written for the public market. It was presumably intended for a Church province, maybe for the Church everywhere. The Lukan writings seem to be written primarily for individual, cultivated Christians but probably for cultural outsiders as well. The Gospel of John gives the impression of having been designed for communities in the Johannine Church province.

Why this remarkable writing? To some extent it *may* have happened by accident: local conditions in the community where the first of the evangelists wrote or the personal qualities of the evangelist may have occasioned the writing of the first Gospel. With the model given and the first literary attempt made, the undertaking was copied by more men in Early Christianity. It is also a striking fact that the synoptics belong together. They are not three independent eruptions of creativity; they have some cause in common.

The fact that time went on was also a factor, in itself. "The beginning" and the first "fathers" thereby got their patina. It is always difficult for the present and the authorities of the present to gain the acknowledgement, prestige and authority of "the fathers" and "the good old days". In this case the personal disciples of Jesus — especially the twelve — had furthermore an immense authority as "eyewitnesses", and because they had the reputation of having been authorized by Jesus himself, the Risen One, and because they had such a position within the Church. It is easy to understand that the death of these pillars and other eyewitnesses sharpened the demand for the legacy to be preserved carefully and committed to writing.

Neither is it impossible that some of these "fathers", Peter for instance, had something to do themselves with the matter. Peter may have given Mark occasion to write, or even urged him to do so, before his own death.

Another "natural" guess is that the progressive institutionalization and consolidation of the Church made it desirable to have better books than before for the different needs of the communities.

Concrete events outside the Church might have played their role as well, especially the fall of Jerusalem and the destruction of the Temple in the year 70 A.D.[77] We know what a catastrophe this was to the Jews and

Hellenism in Jewish Palestine (New York: Jew. Theol. Sem. of Amer., 1950) 83—99. See also the discussion in *The Relationships Among the Gospels. An Interdisciplinary Dialogue* (ed. W.O. Walker, Jr.; San Antonio: Trinity University Press, 1978) 123—92.
[77] Cf. Kelber, *Oral* 210—11.

what strivings for consolidation it evoked. The Christian sources do not give us reason for believing that the fate of Jerusalem in the year 70 shaked Early Christianity as much as Judaism, but it is reasonable to presume (1) that even those Jews who had become Christians were influenced by this catastrophe and its immediate consequences: the holy city and the Temple could no longer be what they had been; (2) that the Palestinian authorities of Early Christianity could no longer have the same influence as before in the Church while other Christian centres gained greater influence; (3) that the fact that *Judaism* after the fall of the Temple consolidated itself hastened Early Christianity's consolidation with defence and contra-attacks against the mother-religion. In these ways the fate of Jerusalem and the Temple may have effected the work with the Jesus-tradition in Christian centres and contributed to the origin of solid, written Gospels.

3.3.4.9. The polyphonic character of the written Gospel

The Early Church was not only a number of independent congregations. There was also a common sense of unity: we are the Church of Christ. A sign of this is the fact that the Gospels were so quickly distributed to other communities. They were *commune bonum* for the Christians.

A classical point in the discussion about the Fourth Gospel is the question of whether this Gospel was written to complete the other Gospels or to replace them. This question is, however, pertinent for each one of the synoptic Gospels as well. And it is important: Was this book written in order to be *the* Gospel in a community or was it written in order to function as one of many voices in a choir? Only if we know for sure that an evangelist intends his book to be the exclusive Gospel for his community can we take his book as a full presentation of his own total view. If he was writing in order to enrich existing collections and/or Gospels, it is not unlikely that he could *presuppose* very much and allow himself a one-sidedness in his selection of material and in his accentuations which he might otherwise have avoided.

Let me just hint at a few points. In the Gospel of *John* we easily see which disciple is the ideal one in the Johannine Church: "the Beloved Disciple". But Peter and the twelve are not rejected. We may suspect criticism against them, but their authority is respected. We get a similar impression in the notices in 20:30—31, and 21:24—25, the words about the selection the evangelist has made from the Jesus-tradition. Nothing here indicates that the Gospel of John is intended to be the only acceptable Gospel. The spirit in these notices is not exclusive. The Gospel of John has not come to displace but to complete the others.

In the *Lukan* prologue we cannot read for sure any criticism against Luke's predecessors. If Luke reproaches them, he does so in an almost indiscernible way. He reveals no wish to displace other Gospels. What he says clearly is that his book will fulfil a special function which obviously the other "orderly accounts" he knows cannot fulfil. The Lukan writings are intended to be used as a complement to other Gospels. Therefore, we cannot presume that Luke presents everything he accepts concerning Jesus in his Gospel.

The author of the *Matthean* Gospel does not say one explicit word about himself and his informants. In the finale of the book (28:16—20) we read, however, that Jesus gives his disciples the command to teach all nations "to observe all that I have commanded you". Certainly this has in view not only sayings of Jesus of a commanding character but the authoritative Jesus-tradition in its entirety. We get the impression that the Gospel of Matthew is intended to be as complete as possible when it goes about the concrete Jesus-tradition. It shall be an all-comprehensive instrument for all tasks which the Risen One has given his Church. On the other hand, it is not likely that Matthew thinks he has collected "everything" in his book and that, therefore, this Gospel shall replace the other collections of Jesus-tradition. We can see how Matthew uses the Gospel of Mark (I think he does). The latter is almost totally swallowed up; the *material* in the book of Mark becomes almost superfluous now. The same applies to the Q-collection. But, even though Matthew reworks his two main sources in this way, he treats the material in them with a striking respect. Nowhere does he reveal suspicion or negativism against his sources or their authors. Therefore he certainly has not wanted to silence the oral tradition, refute the older collections or dispatch the Gospel of Mark to the *geniza*. The Gospel of Matthew is not written in an exclusive spirit. The evangelist stood in a tradition, in which Kings and Chronicles could stand side by side and a scriptural verse could be interpreted in many ways by one and the same teacher. Matthew certainly would not mind that the vivid Gospel of Mark was used even in the future.[78]

It is not easy to know, how *Mark* thought of earlier materials concerning the words and deeds of Jesus. Like Matthew, he finds no need to say a word about himself or his work. For my part I think that Mark has no intention to write a complete account of Jesus' words and deeds — "all about Jesus" — or to replace other attempts. Nor do I believe the many

[78] The fact that the Gospel of Mark actually did come in the shadow of Matthew's Gospel, is another matter.

new hypotheses about his severe polemics against the family of Jesus, the twelve, Early Christian prophets and whatever.[79] To me it seems probable that Mark knows about the Q-collection and *respects it*. Nothing indicates that Mark was so abnormal that he held the sayings of Jesus in contempt. He simply makes a narrow selection. The limited space he gives the sayings material in his book (some 27% of the total text) might very well have the explanation that there already existed a good and respectable collection which Mark neither wanted to integrate into his own presentation nor to replace. If the abrupt ending of Mark's Gospel is not due to some external, accidental fact — that one or two leaves are missing or that the evangelist's work was interrupted or that he wanted to write one more volume like Luke without being able to do so — it might have the explanation that the resurrection narratives were very well known texts, which perhaps even had a prominent place in the eucharistic liturgy. This is a hypothetical guess but hardly more far-fetched than a lot of other arguments from silence concerning the Gospel of Mark.

The synoptic Gospels have a very simple canon history. This is easy to explain. They were rooted in the same tradition: they stemmed from circles whose members obviously knew each other rather well; as literary works they originated in connection with each other and were not written in order to displace each other. It was only natural that in many congregations they were added to one another immediately in the beginning. The fact that they seem to have got a "flying start" in the Church and an uncontested authority from the very beginning, presumably means that they came from leading Christian authorities and centres. In the competition with other "orderly accounts" they were victorious; the fight was scarcely hard. It was a matter of "the survival of the fittest" but also dependent on certain privileges: these three did not have to fight each for himself; they belonged together and had a common authority.

The written gospel of the Church is a polyphonic gospel — or tetraphonic gospel. This is not an entirely secondary fact, simply due to the recording of the gospel tradition and the inclusion of four records in a canon. To some extent it is even founded in the fact that the oral gospel tradition *intra muros ecclesiae* was a plurality with a considerable homogeneity, and the fact that the evangelists did not intend to silence each other. It soon became difficult in the Church to keep the witnesses of the different evangelists apart.[80] This is irritating to us New Testament

[79] Thus Kelber, *Oral* esp. 90—105 with references.
[80] Cf. H. Merkel, *Die Pluralität der Evangelien als theologisches und exegetisches Problem in der Alten Kirche* (Traditio christiana 3; Bern & Frankfurt a.M.: Lang, 1978).

scholars today, when we work hard in order to see the distinctive profile of the different books as clearly as possible. But the four evangelists could certainly have written as Paul did: "Whether then it is I or they, so we preach and so you believed" (1 Cor 15:11).[81]

3.3.4.10. Holy writ and viva vox

The spoken and the written word both have their advantages and their disadvantages. This subject is very fascinating. From before the era of perfectly printed books and rapid, silent reading, we have many utterances on this problem. Well known are Plato's words about the stupid written book, which can do nothing but repeat the same words, and the early Christian fathers' appreciative testimonies about the living voice in contrast to books.[82] Martin Luther took up this theme in a remarkable way, insisting on the principle that the gospel (das Evangelium) is not holy scriptures but a living, sounding word: *viva vox*.[83]

In this paper I have rejected much in Werner Kelber's book, *The Oral and the Written Gospel*. His approach is based on an all too simple contrast between the spoken and the written word, between orality and written delivery (textuality). Nonetheless, I think his mobilizing of observations from Anglo-American folkloristic studies of "orality" — particularly if this category is taken in a more pluralistic form[84] — is valuable: from here the New Testament debate can be vitalized in questions concerning the gospel tradition and hermeneutics. In fact, Kelber's ambition is not only to elucidate the relation between the oral and the written gospel, but also, at the same time, to clarify the "oral psycho-dynamics" and to work out an "oral hermeneutic" as a complement to the usual hermeneutic which he calls a textual one.

I cannot follow Kelber very far in these points either. Yet, I think his subjects are important. Jesus and Early Christianity presented their

---

[81] Cf. the attitude expressed in Phil 1:18.

[82] Plato, Phaedros 274b—78a; cf. epist. II (314) and VII (340—42). On different aspects of the problem of oral and written delivery in antiquity and in the Ancient Church, see H. Frhr. von Campenhausen, *Kirchliches Amt und geistliche Vollmacht in den ersten drei Jahrhunderten* (BHT 14; Tübingen: Mohr, 1953) 221—33, L. Vischer, Die Rechtfertigung der Schriftstellerei in der Alten Kirche, *TZ* 12 (1956) 320—36, E.F. Osborn, Teaching and Writing in the First Chapter of the *Stromateis* of Clement of Alexandria, *JTS* NS 10 (1959) 335—43, and H. Karpp, Viva vox, Mullus (Festschrift T. Klauser, *JAC* Erg-bd 1; Münster i. W.: Achendorff, 1964) 190—98. Cf. also n. 37 above.

[83] See R. Prenter, *Spiritus creator. Studier i Luthers theologi* (2nd ed.; Copenhagen: Samlerens Forlag, 1946) 127—37.

[84] A good example is R. Finnegan, *Oral Poetry. Its nature, significance and social context* (Cambridge: Cambridge University Press; London, New York, Melbourne, 1977).

own, new, specific message — from the eruptive centre of their "inner tradition" — in oral forms first of all, and did so in a cultural setting where writings were never far away. This means that the transition to a stage where the oral gospel had basically become one or many books was not a superficial, technical triviality. Granted this significant change did not occur immediately when the Gospels were written (the oral tradition and the oral activity in other forms continued), something had started, however, which in the long run would have important consequences. One hundred years later or so the written Gospels had attained the position as holy scriptures and as primary sources for the Christian message. This process is a captivating object for historical study. But it also has deep theological and existential implications. It concerns themes that are among the greatest realities of the Church: law and gospel, holy writ and *viva vox evangelii.*